CHARSLE
SIMON R

KU-498-314

Wedding cakes
and cultural history

Simon R. Charsley

London and New York

First published in 1992
by Routledge
11 New Fetter Lane, London EC4P 4EE

Simultaneously published in the USA and Canada by
Routledge
a division of Routledge, Chapman and Hall Inc.
29 West 35th Street, New York, NY 10001

© 1992 Simon R. Charsley

Typeset by NWL Editorial Services

Printed and bound in Great Britain by
Mackays of Chatham PLC, Chatham, Kent

British Library Cataloguing in Publication Data
A catalogue record for this book is available
from the British Library.

Library of Congress Cataloging in Publication Data
Charsley, S.R.
Wedding cakes and cultural history / by Simon R. Charsley
p. cm.
1. Wedding cakes – Great Britain – History. 2. Wedding
cakes – Great Britain – Social aspects. 3. Wedding cakes –
History. 4. Wedding cakes – Social aspects. I. Title.
GT2797.C44 1992   91-24278
392'.5 – dc20   CIP

ISBN 0–415–02648–2 (hbk)
       0–415–02649–0 (pbk)

Contents

Part II   The making of the British wedding cake

Part III   Users, uses and meanings

Illustrations

Foreword

I have often thought that wedding parties ought to be held five years after taking the vows, if for no other reason than to celebrate the fact that the happy nuptials managed to stick it out that long. The survival of romance should have its rewards, and much champagne and cake would not seem so needlessly squandered. For better or for worse, the cynic's smile has no effect on love, and as Simon Charsley has so thoroughly elucidated in this book, the Great Cake and its layers upon layers of sublimated meanings – erotic to commemorative – are certainly here to stay. It is a food that has become a veritable institution. A wedding without it would be a wedding without protocol, a rite without confirmation.

Mary Douglas's apt observation on this very point several years ago, tossed out as a challenge to food research, has indeed found its realisation in this rather exhaustive analysis of the British – and by extension, the American and European – roots of the wedding cake tradition. I am particularly impressed by the way Dr Charsley has used history to support sociology and put them to work for something I call 'culinary anthropology'. In short, this is a deeply insightful, profusely documented foray into the wedding cake in its broadest sense. It anticipates a new kind of food study that (at long last!) begins to view food as part of a holistic world, a world where history and myth, recipe and performance, change and continuity are actually seen as one.

William Woys Weaver
University of Pennsylvania
Philadelphia

Preface

The history of confectionery and baking is unlikely territory for a social anthropologist. I might explain that cake-making and decorating have always been my secret passion, that I am therefore better qualified to write the present small study than may at first be supposed. I might but I cannot, for it would be untrue. The topic was initially a tempting byway, or perhaps a sunny, time-encrusted corner of a charming garden in which to relax from the more strenuous work of a student of contemporary societies. I hope the reader will agree that it turned out to be something more than that, but still there is no way in which I can claim the product to be the definitive study: an essay merely.

To the extent that I have avoided the elementary errors which always go with a lack of practical experience, the chief credit has to be given to Jean Hutton, my wife. She has not only baked and decorated as I have not, but is an historian as well. She has listened patiently to real and imagined discoveries over the years, as the study was intermittently pursued. With her I was able to discuss most aspects of the book as it developed.

There are many others also on whose assistance I have been grateful to be able to call. Above all I have to thank William Woys Weaver for the very material help and encouragement he so readily and generously provided for the study and for agreeing to endorse the result with his kind Foreword. Bridget Ann Henisch has likewise helped and encouraged, both personally and through her own excellent books on medieval food and on the Twelfth cake. The latter is in many ways the wedding cake's direct predecessor. Others to whom I am similarly grateful include Alan Littlewood – who has also kindly let me quote one of his excellent recipes, Robert Robertson, Barbara Santich, Walter Edwards, Hervé LeGrand, Margaret McKay and Margaret Kenna. The owners and staff of numerous bakers and confectioners, and the many

others who so willingly participated in the Glasgow marrying study from
which all this began, deserve profuse thanks too. I have finally to crown
the list with the names of Professors David Schneider and Adam Kuper.
Without their initial interest and support this enterprise would not have
got under way at all.

For institutional support I have to thank the Economic and Social
Research Council (ESRC) who funded the Glasgow study already
published as *Rites of Marrying: the Wedding Industry in Scotland*
(Manchester University Press, 1991). My own university and depart-
ment provided the support needed for the subsequent more specialised
work. Amongst the libraries and librarians to whom I owe a debt of
gratitude, the National Library of Scotland with its McAdam collection
of materials on bakery and confectionery deserves special mention.

Permissions from the Royal Anthropological Institute of Great
Britain and Ireland to reprint material from my article 'Interpretation
and custom: the case of the wedding cake' (*Man* 22: 93–100), and from
the Folklore Society similarly for 'The wedding cake: history and
meanings' (*Folklore* IC: 232–41), are both gratefully acknowledged.

Simon Charsley
Glasgow
May 1991

Introduction

When I began working on the wedding cake in the early 1980s the problem appeared to be the persistence of something timeless, a complicated cultural object taken for granted to the extent that its extraordinary form was scarcely ever questioned. By 1990 when this book was finally being written, though the old order had by no means been swept away, a radical change was under way. At the beginning cultural change had predominantly to be reconstructed from recorded minutiae of the past. The results of such work are still of great interest and allow lessons about the cultural long run to be drawn. But by now there is a resumption of spectacular change to be examined too, as it is occurring. The study is in consequence more difficult to complete; its matter provides a constant reminder that processes of cultural change never are concluded.

The wedding cake, whether 'traditional' or in new styles, is no ordinary object. Mary Douglas picked it out in a lecture in 1974 as conspicuously likely to attract the attention of 'a competent young anthropologist arriving on this planet from Mars'. At the weddings to which he was likely to be invited he would, she suggested with an exaggeration which is almost legitimate, 'be perhaps baffled to make up his mind whether the central focus of the ceremony was the marriage or the cake'. In the same vein she asserted that the ceremonial of kava in the island of Tonga or tea in Japan 'would pale into insignificance compared with the ceremonial surrounding the cutting and distribution of the wedding cake' (Douglas 1982: 105). The extent to which such claims are justified will emerge in succeeding chapters; immediately however, it is clear that she was correct and perceptive in picking out the cake, as extraordinary as it is familiar, as a prime object for study.

For her the essential strategy of such a study would be to set this cake within the system of which she sees it as being a part, the British food system. Such a system is a set of rules generating patterns – she was later to imagine such rules as the instructions in a computer program (Douglas 1984) – the object of this structuralist style of analysis being to detect patterns and explain them in terms of rules.[1] The patterns would be formed by the foods to be offered together or kept separate, in succession as parts of a meal, on different occasions in the course of a day, over longer calendrical periods, and even over lifetimes. And by belonging to such a system, the contention is that foods acquire their meanings. They may represent each other within the system of alternatives and equivalences and they may represent the events, the meals and the occasions in which they appear. Her reasoning leads her to assert that the wedding cake 'can be presented plausibly' as a pile of biscuits. This is not, as it might appear to be, to devalue the cake, for the humble and characteristically cheap biscuit is for her very special in the British food system. It is 'a condensed symbol of all the food events and the social events of a day and a week and a lifetime' (Douglas 1982: 112–13). When it comes to considering 'food as an art form', this becomes a matter of relating one system to another, the food system with the aesthetic.

This is very different to the perspective of the present work but since it constitutes by far the most extensive body of anthropological thought hitherto applied to wedding cakes, and comes from one of the most influential and respected practitioners in the field, it is necessary to explain why the lead which she offers is not followed here. It seems to me to be based on a mistake of the kind which generates metaphysics, quickly losing touch with the realities of human lives in history.

'System', first, is a word well calculated to mislead. In common use it can refer to any amount of regular interconnection. If cakes invariably appear at weddings, there is a system here; if cakes are white and brides' dresses are white, there is a system here. In this sense it is undeniable that life is full of system; there are a mass of *de facto* interconnections and they arise from a variety of sources of kinds which will be explored in this book. There is an empirical basis for Douglas's claim to have identified system here. It is Nicod's study of patterns of eating in four working-class families in different parts of England, with each of whom he stayed for a month or more (Douglas & Nicod 1974). The uncontentious starting point is the assertion that each had a food system, 'a family food system'. Because a single pattern could be identified in these four cases and appeared to be quite general in the streets in which they lived, Douglas moves on to ascribe it to the working class as a whole. A further small step makes it the British food system. More concretely, the part that biscuits are identified as playing in the routines of eating in four households becomes an explanation of the

British enthusiasm for biscuits, an explanation in terms of their meaning within the food system identified. The standard British wedding cake becomes a special form of biscuit. It is thus placed within the system and its meaning explained.

There is already a dubious generalising progression here, explaining the whole by the part in a way which ought to be surprising for anyone of structuralist inclinations, as well as leaving behind any concern with the date and all other particularities of the original observations. It is what is happening to 'system' in the course of the argument which is more fundamental however. When 'system' begins to be imagined more rigorously, the kind of mistake which founds metaphysics is made. To identify 'the food system', or other similar systems at whatever level, is to move to something of more apparent moment than *de facto* interconnections, to discover what seems to be a new level of reality. It suggests at least a coherence within a more extensive set of inter-connections, and the existence of principles on which this coherence is based. It suggests boundaries, so that one such system can relate to another and perhaps be compared with it. It suggests something which exists and even has power, whether or not those who are represented as being within its power are aware of it (e.g. Douglas 1975: 273). Like Van Gennep's famous scheme of rites of passage which provides a prototype of structuralist thinking (Leach 1976), it appears to offer a way in which an observer with the key can tell people what they are doing and why they are doing it. Such a revelation can be confidently asserted in the face of professions of ignorance from those performing the actions and even of their determined disbelief.

The identification of system underlying practice has another basis of plausibility. People do sometimes devise systems of considerable complexity based on principles. They sometimes, as in the law, work to systematise inherently unruly events. System, that is to say, is a human value as well as a concept. As such it is ethnographically and individu-ally variable, and, when applied to human affairs, often more a matter of aspiration than of achievement. In the past it was perhaps most highly developed in the spectacular but specialised field of mathematics, but more recently the computer has boosted the aspirations of systematising thought to encompass ever-widening areas of everyday life. Computer programs have also provided appealing models of system, being able to generate great apparent complexity out of simple rules.

System in more ambitious senses is therefore in the air, in contemporary western culture at least, but this does not mean that any underlying reality of this kind shapes human practice where it has not been made and designed by particular humans to do so. For practices which have grown up piecemeal, as are the practices surrounding food and popular rites, there should be no reason to imagine that they are as a whole part of or manifestations of any system, even if a confusion of thought sometimes leads people in that direction (cf. Firth 1973: 260–1; Goody 1982: 26–7, 29–32).

Here the system idea is made more plausible by attaching it to 'food', one of those terms which seem so basic to English-speakers that anthropologists are inclined to use them as anchors in the designation of fields for cross-cultural study. It is, however, again an ethno-graphically complex and variable term. This makes it a good starting point for many kinds of enquiry into ideas and practices in the fields of production, consumption, nutrition and taste (e.g. Richards 1939; Goody 1982; Mennell 1985), but not a suitable *a priori* discriminant of what is to be within 'the' system and what is to be excluded. If it is so used it becomes a part of somebody's attempt to impose system on ranges of human thought and activity which, unless they have been devised as a system, display it to the disbelieving eye only intermittently.

As far as the wedding cake is concerned, those who have them may think of them as food, since they are or contain cake, in Britain at least, and cake is recognised as a kind of food. But they are also confectionery, which allies them with sweets and chocolate which are not generally thought of as food. As will be seen, it is not even to be taken for granted that being eaten is a leading characteristic of this peculiar 'cake'. As a Belgian writer on the history of confectionery notes: 'ces pièces somptueuses figurent sur la table et échappent à l'appetit des invités' (Vanaise 1928: 29). It tests the boundaries of 'food' and raises a problem which is skirted even by Goody (1982) in his wide-ranging comparative study of cooking and cuisine, the problem raised by the non-nutritional use of objects which could be food (Garine 1976: 150). Certainly, the British cake contrasts with its continental cousins in its separation from the food of the wedding feast. In America its marginal nature as food is very apparent even in Douglas's own study of *Food in the Social Order* (1984: 207): in the particular context being examined there it is treated merely as marking the event at which it appears as a wedding.

The idea that the wedding cake is properly to be understood or its meaning elucidated by placing it within the food system is therefore less than, as Douglas might say, plausible. It is not surprising that the results of the application of such a method are also amongst the oddest findings of anthropology. Douglas explains that 'The icing of the wedding cake is able to express what it does because it is at the pinnacle of a very rigorously formalized set of rules which segregate liquid from solid with

complete consistency right through all the constituent food occasions.'
The cake itself 'is a sweet cereal confection on which a white liquid
dressing has been poured, but the dressing has set into the hardest,
shiniest and most improbably patterned crust' (Douglas 1982: 113;
Douglas & Nicod 1974: 746–7).

The present study is, in contrast, not a study of systems and rules but
of cultural creativity. It shares the theoretical standpoint of Goody's
study already referred to, despite its relatively minute scope and range.
It means to echo his dismissal of exclusivist claims of functionalist,
structuralist and other predecessors, and asserts that there cannot be a
choice between culture and practical reason (Sahlins 1976) or any
primacy attached to atemporal abstractions like culture or structure.
Every enterprise is culturally informed, meaning that it is formulated in
relation to values and understandings as they are drawn from their past
experience by those involved. It has then to be carried out in a world of
practical possibilities and constraints grounded in factors over which
those concerned have no control. It is necessarily the outcome of such
interactions which shapes culture, in a continuing process, as well as
altering the practical possibilities and constraints for future action in
tiny or occasionally substantial ways. The understanding of change over
time is therefore not something extra, a desirable bonus to add to
synchronic study; it is essential if the nature of human culture is not to
be grossly misunderstood.

Every cake made has therefore to be understood as representing past
cultural creativity as the material for future creation. From a
contemporary perspective it appears as a single, timeless 'thing' within
the taken-for-granted repertoire of a particular culture; yet it is the
product of a complex, contingent and continuing history. The part it
plays in a major rite of contemporary life is known to all; yet rationales
of any kind are rare. It makes sense to all involved with it; yet whether it
has meaning of any kind is commonly doubted. It may, as has been said,
be regarded as a food; yet it is not consumed for its nutritional value nor
even, often, for the pleasure of its eating. It is expensive, but not a luxury;
indeed it is a practical necessity for most of the three-quarters of a
million people, in Britain alone, who get married each year.

Such near paradoxes crowd around the wedding cake. This book uses
their elucidation in a particular context as a route into the discussion of
wider issues: of the cultural nexus between past and present, the
significance of interpretation for change, and in general of the principles
and phenomena of cultural change. Underlying it is a concern with
displaying the relevance for anthropological thinking of detailed
cultural enquiries in western societies. The literacy of the culture to

which the wedding cake throughout its history has belonged is what
equips it with evidence valuable and exciting to an anthropologist. The
half-sightedness of anthropology's classic synchronic stance, which
many have sought to overcome by a renewed interest in history, can here
be decisively improved. The past, even of the taken-for-granted, has
been at least in some measure documented.

But there is something more special too. Food, drink and
confectionery and their development in Europe, in particular the
preparation of so complex an item as the wedding cake, are peculiarly
instructive. Unlike most other kinds of material object which, once
created, have an indefinite life and may stay around as anchors for
subsequent nostalgia (Shaw & Chase 1989: 4), such items of
consumption are created and destroyed in a reproductive cycle as short
as those of the smaller living species. They therefore may 'evolve' on a
time scale that can readily be encompassed in research and in ways that
have sometimes been minutely charted in the wealth of recipes recorded
since the late medieval period. In this field at least, the familiar
furnishing of the contemporary world can be observed taking shape.
There can therefore be constructed a base against which to test out old
ideas – the structuralist theories considered above, as well as more
general theories of cultural change – and from which a firmer account
of processes can be developed. The transient incompleteness of the
present, even possibilities for the future, can better be grasped.

This book is therefore an essay on cultural change. Much of its
'fieldwork' was necessarily conducted amongst written records of the
past, but it owes its origins to a study somewhat more conventional for
anthropology, in a more conventional field: Glasgow, Scotland, in the
1980s. This is reported more generally in *Rites of Marrying: the Wedding
Industry in Scotland* (Charsley 1991). Both past and present, like every
anthropological field, had their own advantages and limitations; they
offered particular opportunities and there were particular problems to
be overcome or accepted. And like any other resultant monograph, the
contribution of this one is empirical as well as theoretical. It documents
aspects of culinary history, in the areas of baking and confectionery
particularly. These are still underworked despite their proximity to the
established field of food research, or perhaps because of their
marginality to it. For this reason key texts have been quoted at length.
They are the markers which the present study has located and they
exemplify the chief kinds of data with which it has worked. There will
always be more to be drawn from them. It is hoped particularly that
others with experience of the practicalities of baking and confectionery
will be challenged to make more expert evaluations. But the book's

central concern is a typically anthropological one. It is with the part that attributions of meaning – inevitably meanings in various senses of that term – play in processes of cultural generation and continuity.

Part I
Preliminaries

1 The British wedding cake in the late twentieth century

CAKES IN WEDDINGS

It is as a prop for photographs that the cake features first at most weddings. The standard series of photographs includes 'the cutting of the cake'. This is taken after the ceremony and just before the couple and their supporters are released by the photographer to begin the reception. The cake will have been set up on a stand on a table and provided with a large knife, either silver-handled or at least with its handle wrapped in foil. Stand and cake knife are important items for which hotels and caterers sometimes make separate charges; more often they make a selling point of the fact that they are not doing so. The bouquets which the bride and bridesmaids have earlier been carrying are arranged around the cake. For the photograph, bride and groom are marshalled into position, together holding the knife with its blade resting on the icing of the bottom tier. Both look at the camera; they do not cut. Others may or may not be included in the picture.

Once the photographer has relinquished control of the couple, the involvement of the company as a whole in the event begins. It may begin with the 'real' cutting of the cake, but very often the cake is simply abandoned at this stage, standing to one side and attracting no interest at all while the guests are greeted. In the more formal pattern, followed generally in Scotland, the 'line-up' takes place. The bridal party stand in line to greet the entire company individually as they pass down the line kissing, congratulating and briefly chatting.

When the second 'cake-cutting' is finally reached, bride and groom once again hold the knife jointly, with the company gathered round to watch unless they are already seated at table for a formal meal. Bride and groom force the knife into the cake and attempt to slice through to the outside. This is often difficult with a professionally made cake and impossible with an amateur. Getting the icing hard enough to support the pillars carrying the weight of the upper tiers without being so hard as to be uncuttable is a well-known technical problem. But complete failure is inconceivable and any measure of success is greeted with applause. A toast to the bride and groom is then given, in the Scottish pattern by the man who is to be master of ceremonies at the meal. In a church marriage this is commonly the celebrant (Charsley 1991: 157).

Thereafter the cake, or at least its bottom tier, is taken away for a third and at last effective cutting. It reappears in tiny portions for consumption by the company. If they are sitting down for a meal, the pieces may be distributed to everyone; otherwise they will simply be available for those who care to take them. Some will always declare their dislike for wedding cake, and nothing is in any case made of the eating, either by the couple or the guests. A bottom tier provides between eighty and one hundred and twenty slices. This is adequate for most receptions without the middle or upper tiers having to be used at all. Some may wrap pieces to take home, with jokes – from grandmothers – about putting them under their pillows to dream of the one they will marry.

In the Scottish wedding, inedible ornaments on the cake are called 'favours'. They and the decoration from the top are removed from the cake and, together with bouquets and table flowers, distributed in the course of the evening by bride and bridesmaids to the women amongst the guests. This is done with an elaborate and often carefully worked-out system of priorities. Usually every woman at the wedding will receive a favour of some kind. The number that can reasonably be put on the cake is frequently inadequate for this; extras will then have been bought in and they will be used in the same way but without ever going near the cake.

At the end of the reception, the cake remaining is taken home by the families of the couple. The top tier is often retained intact. Whatever is left of the others is used for sending in small, specially printed wedding-cake boxes to people who were unable to be at the wedding. These may be people who gave presents but were not invited, as well as those invited who could not attend. Residues normally end up with the couple and are offered to their visitors, sometimes for months afterwards. The top tier is often said to be 'for the christening'. Couples not wishing to anticipate any such event may well use it for some other occasion, a house-warming party or a parents' silver wedding perhaps.

The cake is important in many weddings therefore in making possible a whole series of events. Without it, an essential photograph, the cutting and the toast, and having not only cake but in Scotland also favours to distribute at the wedding and afterwards, would all fall away. But this is to suggest an importance far more derivative than is really appropriate. The cake is a primary element of the contemporary British wedding.

Whatever other rites and formalities may be omitted in the celebration of a marriage, a cake to be cut is the least likely to be.

THEIR FORM AND RANGES OF VARIATION

What is this wedding cake? A major change may well have been creeping in as the 1980s drew to a close – this is discussed in the next section – but up till then there had been no difficulty in providing a rather detailed specification. There was, that is to say, no difference of opinion on the matter. At most, people might occasionally hold back a little from committing themselves to it by referring to it as 'the traditional wedding cake' with some implication that there might be others. What they would be referring to was a construction of three large cakes, or 'tiers' as they were always called. These were arranged in declining size one above the other. The cakes themselves were of a dark, rich-fruit mixture, not of any fixed recipe but generally thought of as distinctive. The tiers of the cake would match; each was covered with almond paste and then iced with a smooth white icing. This was built up in layers and had a more or less elaborate piped decoration applied on its surface, also in icing. The upper tiers were supported by pillars. Further but inedible ornaments were attached to the individual cakes, mostly on the sides, and a decoration was placed on the very top. This might be a miniature bride and groom, a confection of artificial flowers and feathers, or a small vase of flowers, real or artificial. The other ornaments were of two kinds, either silver or gold plastic horseshoes, slippers, etc., or small confections made up of artificial flowers, ribbons and the like. These, but particularly the latter, were in Scotland the 'favours' already mentioned. Anyone might make such a cake but there were practical problems which put it beyond the range of most home bakers.

Such a specification was generally accepted. It had never meant, however, that any absolute conformity was required. A small survey in 1990 suggested that almost 90 per cent of commercial cakes were still made entirely with a rich-fruit mixture,[1] though couples who did not like wedding cake, as it was usually put, could have a different top tier, most often sponge, or even an alternative for the whole cake. Three tiers were not essential: in 1982 the leading West of Scotland wedding-cake manufacturer, selling well over a thousand cakes a year, produced 30 per cent which did not have three tiers: 1 per cent had four, 7 per cent only one, and the remainder two. Whatever the combination, it was composed of standard 'bottoms', 'middles' and 'tops'. In the less affluent 1930s, their commonest cake had two tiers but the specification, with three tiers, was already identical.

Colours might diverge from 'virginal white', as the manager of the same company put it, either for all the icing or just for the edging and other decoration. Strong colours were available: two red cakes, one 'apple green' and one 'autumn gold' were supplied during the year. The manager commented that they had not yet been asked for black. In general though, the colours chosen represented no more than pale and modest divergences from white. Pink was by far the most popular, followed by blue. Lemon, lilac and peach, cream and mauve were other possibilities. Coloured cakes accounted for only 18 per cent of the output. As regards shape, this company offered only round or square, though hexagonal cakes were also made in Glasgow and other more eccentric shapes could be imported from England. The tiers could be mounted without pillars, but this was very rare.

Such variants in shape and colour were often regarded as modern innovations, but this was in the first place merely a strategy for reconciling observable variation with the presence of an acknowledged norm. Confectioners' brochures from the 1930s show that precisely the same kinds of 'innovation' were being offered then, though probably to a smaller but more affluent section of the population. Acceptable variation does, however, offer scope for future development in the specification itself. Trends of choice may then cumulate into changed expectations. The square cake, possible but unusual in the 1930s, was being ordered by 60 per cent of customers in the early 1980s, was what would be chosen to illustrate wedding articles in magazines and for the covers of wedding books, and was well on the way to becoming the new norm.

THE CHANGING TRADE IN THE 1980s

Despite some falling away of the number of weddings, the wedding trades in general – the dress shops, car hirers, photographers and video-makers, florists, stationers, hoteliers and caterers – burgeoned during the increasingly affluent 1980s (Charsley 1991).

For the cake trade, however, it was a complicated decade, with a major change, invisible at its beginning, sweeping the country by its end. It was complicated because there were four elements intertwining within it. For a start, the old specification was not abandoned but a number of enthusiastic specialist confectioners around the country exploited the opportunities of affluence to produce bigger and better. New styles of icing were developed, using an increasing variety of techniques, and the intricate and therefore costly designs of earlier periods were sometimes copied (MacGregor 1988). The height of cakes, however, is the clearest pointer here. At the beginning of the 1980s, as has been seen, four-tier cakes were rare and were generally regarded as the ultimate. By the end of it, specialist firms at the top end of the market were making five-tiers as features for their displays, pricing them generously – in one recorded case at £500 when a three-tier could still be had locally for under £100 – and finding them selling. Some firms reported selling cakes with seven and even eight tiers. Larger cakes retained a rarity value – three tiers remained by far the commonest – but what was needed to make an impression was escalating as the decade wore on.

The three-tier standard was, however, under perhaps more serious attack from a different quarter. At the beginning of the decade most cakes had three tiers and if customers could not rise to three it would be two, with singles making up a small residue only, but by the end of it the demand for singles had picked up. Suppliers were often selling more singles than two-tiers, though not all were happy with this trend. One proprietor encountered was insisting on a minimum of two tiers as essential for anything to be properly called a wedding cake – and to justify the kind of price tag which the workmanship expected for such a cake would require. The reason for the trend was not altogether clear. It could have been in part an increasing polarisation of wealth and poverty in the society at large: as well as more huge and lavish weddings, more small and economical ones may have been being held, but I have no direct evidence of this. More likely, it was mainly to do with adjusting to the prevalence of second and subsequent weddings – more than one in three and rising over the decade – and the new styles of cake on offer. Few weddings of any kind would take place without a cake, but it might not be felt necessary to go through the full procedure with a multi-tiered traditional cake again after the first time.

The effect of these first two strands of change was to widen the scope for choice, and a third is the prevalence of deliberate efforts on the part of suppliers to achieve the same effect. It was a decade of considerable experimentation. The expectation that cakes would be, at least for the base icing, white was weakening. Pale colours became common as the decade wore on, with ivory so popular by the end of it that ornament makers were beginning to offer their top pieces in that shade as well as in white. Some firms were prepared to match the cake to the dress, but for one firm at least, this proved more trouble than it was worth; too often it generated not the intended satisfaction but complaints that the shade achieved was too light or too dark. Shapes other than square and round, and more different shapes, came to be on offer widely, and to be sold. New ways of assembling tiers were also appearing. One Scottish firm had, and occasionally sold, a model with three cakes of equal size arranged as steps. The front of each rested on the step below, the back was supported on pillars. A red carpet was laid down the steps and a model bride and groom stood at the top. A construction described – not unreasonably – as American was also sometimes seen. This involved a direct stacking of smaller cake on larger, or perhaps two stacked tiers on top raised on tall pillars above a larger base. Continental styles – also discussed in the following chapter – began to be imported more often too, as patisseries sometimes entered the wedding market in larger centres.

The fourth strand in the developments of the 1980s was in a sense merely a further expansion of choice, but its scale and implications are such that it deserves to be treated separately. This was the revival of interest in sugarpaste and the rise of the sugarcraft movement. 'Sugarpaste' covers here a variety of preparations which provide a plastic sugar substance which can be rolled out, cut, moulded and coloured, and in general used as a covering and modelling medium. In some forms it goes back to medieval times but, as will emerge in a later chapter, since the late nineteenth century it had in Britain been eclipsed as a decorative material by the simpler royal icing, piped. It returned in the 1980s to provide a different and in many ways more flexible medium for cake decoration, in the process giving a great impetus to this as a leisure activity. As a covering sugarpaste would be rolled out and draped over the cake, allowing irregular and rounded shapes to be covered in a way that is difficult or impossible using smooth royal icing. The surface could then be decorated in various novel ways, as well as by piping in the old style. The modelling of delicate and highly realistic flowers was a particular focus for enthusiasm and skill and these might be extensively and expensively employed on the grander cakes in the new style.

Such cakes might still be built up with pillars in the old way and they might still use a standard rich-fruit mixture, but one spectacular change was opening the way for others. Sugarpaste cakes were still normally of declining size, one raised above another, but this was often not a vertical pile on pillars. Instead, each separate cake was offset on a stand, usually of a spiral form. The unity of 'the cake' was in this way beginning to break down. The departure might be justified with the idea that sugarpaste lacked the strength to carry the weight of upper tiers, but, as the continuing presence of traditionally tiered cakes proved, this was only partially true or relevant. Implications for cake decorations were clear too, in Scotland amounting even to a challenge to the favours. At least in the initial enthusiasm generated by the new style, cakes were perceived as decoratively complete, without the expanses of flat, usually white surface which made royal-iced cakes vehicles for the elaborate little confections given away as favours. One leading Scottish specialist expressed the hope that the new style would not be the end of so distinctive a Scottish custom. He clearly could not feel altogether confident in their future though. He was perhaps not helping it by importing his own favours 'direct from Taiwan', rather than buying them from the several active Scottish companies producing them.

The new style affected the shape of the industry too. One after another, suppliers felt that they would have to include sugarpaste in their range; colleges of baking and confectionery began to include it in their syllabuses; but its implications were more radical still. Whereas wedding cake production had previously generally been a sideline of the general baker and confectioner, if sometimes a highly prestigious and visible one, sugarpaste brought in a whole new set of competitors (cf. Becker 1982: 272 ff.). People, most often women, who had gained skills and interests as amateurs, generally through branches of the British Sugarcraft Guild and perhaps encouraged by the entrepreneurial ethos of the 1980s, went into business as providers of wedding and other celebration cakes. Working initially often from their own homes, their overheads were low, and this, combined with their capacity to offer something different and more personal, put them into a strong position to challenge established suppliers. The old order and the product to which it was adjusted were thus under pressure as the 1990s began. It was at least possible that the end of the era which this book explores was near.

DOES A WEDDING CAKE MEAN ANYTHING?

Interviewer   Do you think the cake means anything?
P, a recently married woman   I don't think so. No, really. Do you?
R, her husband   I don't know where it came from but there's a lot centres around it: cutting the cake, toast to the bride and groom. . . .
P   It seems to be an important bit, but I don't know. . . .
R   It's an important part . . . it's a significant part of the wedding ceremony. As the wedding is a day, the cake has become an important part of it.
Interviewer   Is it tied up with the favours?
P   . . . never thought about it.

This conversation catches exactly the first problem that the cake poses. The husband registers its importance in the proceedings, the wife the fact that very little is ever said about it. It was so standardised and inevitable a part of getting married that few ever thought to question it. The cost of having a cake, in the region of £80 in the early 1980s, was frequently talked about, the point of having one hardly ever.

Those who might have been expected to have expert views on the matter were, in the Glasgow study, scarcely more forthcoming. A hotel manager with a strong wedding trade described the cake as 'symbolic', but no, he had never thought what it symbolised. The manager of the wedding-cake firm already quoted was asked why the cake was so important. It was, he said, the focal point of the wedding before the meal, but maybe for only half an hour. He himself had had a wedding cake both times he had been married: 'no wedding's a wedding without a cake'. But he thought it was 'convention' rather than 'tradition': others have cakes, so you have one too. Thinking about it on the spot – because the interviewer was pushing him to do so – he realised that he had been selling the cakes for years but had never wondered why we had them. Later in the same conversation it became obvious that he was never going to produce any further interpretation of his own. He was then asked whether he did not see a link between the cake and the bride in the way they were got up. He did not disagree with this idea but was not interested in it. What he had thought of, he said, was a church spire, the cake being like a church spire.

One young man, interviewed in the run-up to his wedding, did, however, provide a conspicuous exception. He announced:

> Another thing we're not having is a cake. We don't know if this is actually correct, but someone said the cake symbolised . . . [what it symbolised was incomprehensible originally and on the tape], and cutting the cake was her surrendering her virginity. Very sexist! So that was out the window. And my mother said, 'I can make a cake', but it's not that we couldn't afford a cake; because of that we don't want it.

Later, after the wedding, the bride was also interviewed. She explained that they didn't have a cake. 'Everything to do with weddings has its symbols and meanings.' She didn't know the whole story but a girl who had got married eight years before had told her that when she got married people knew that the cutting of the cake meant the bride losing her virginity – 'the way the groom puts his hand on the bride's, so it's not just her; it's him too. A horrible idea!' So they weren't having a wedding cake. She did think of having another ordinary kind of cake.

Interviewer Are there any other things with meanings like that?
Bride The white dress. The bride proclaiming that she's a virgin,

whereas the groom can wear anything and doesn't have to say anything about himself.

Interviewer Surely the white dress doesn't really mean that nowadays?

She thought it did.

Interpretation therefore was scarce but it was possible. When it did occur it might have striking results. The enquiry beginning here aims to evaluate this situation, to locate attributions of meaning in the history of the cake and to try to understand their place in the evolution both of its physical form and of the uses made of it.

2 How distinctive is the British cake?

EUROPE

Viewed from the European mainland this wedding cake has always seemed a peculiarly English development. In periods of 'anglomania' such as the 1890s in France, it might be viewed with friendly amazement (Suzanne 1894: 232–4). Montagné in his great *Larousse Gastronomique*, originally published just before the Second World War, is more guarded. He identifies it as based on the distinctively English plum cake, by then marginally incorporated into the French and Belgian confectionery range. The wedding cake itself is 'a monumental cake', 'a symbol rather than a delicacy, a tradition handed down from one century to the next, whose origins are lost in the mists of antiquity' (Engl. edn 1961: 205).

If the French, Dutch, Germans, Italians or other continental Europeans were to celebrate marriage with a cake of some kind it would be altogether lighter. It might share in the tendency to rise high and to be relatively large, but the standardisation and specialisation which are such marked features of the British cake developed much more hesitantly.

In France and Belgium there were two main styles. Regarded as the more traditional was a giant croquembouche. This is a cone, wide at the base, built up of small round choux pastries which are filled with confectioner's cream and dipped in hot toffee. As the toffee cools it solidifies, making a light brown glossy construction. This can then be decorated with ribbons and sugared almonds, birds and flowers, and often, for weddings, a small bride-and-groom model on the top. For baptisms, first communions and other events, a similar though probably smaller cake may also be prepared with slightly different decorative motifs. Each guest will be served a number of choux broken out from the whole as a sweet course in the wedding meal. Since the toffee which maintains the structure will soon soften and the whole is liable therefore to sag or even collapse, it is a confection which must be prepared and eaten with as little delay as possible. There will normally be one such cake, its size determined by the number of guests. One Breton pâtissier reported in 1990 that 60 per cent of the cakes he supplied for weddings were croquembouches; ten years earlier it had been 90 per cent. It is possible to use the same construction technique to produce a variety of objects: churches, houses, boats, baskets, bowls, etc. Novelty cakes in this tradition have recently become a possibility for weddings. The same pâtissier reported that 65 per cent of his croquembouche orders were for the basic type since others were 15 per cent more costly.

The other style is less distinctively French but appears in various forms around the Continent. Its basis is a light sponge cake, a Genoa recipe being common. A set of cakes, generally round and of declining size, are prepared. These are flavoured and decorated in a variety of styles with confectioner's cream or fresh cream, commonly laced with fruit liqueurs, or with icing, sometimes decorated with glacéed fruits, or macaroons, or with marzipan or sugarpaste ornaments. Cakes in a set are expected to match. They are set up on a stand, a 'présentoir' in French, with the smallest cake on the top, the largest on the bottom. Stands in the past have normally raised the cakes one above the other in a tapering column, often with a central support cutting through the middle of each cake. Such stands may allow as many as ten layers to be set up.

There are doubtless regional specialities in France and in other countries and regions of Europe. The whole topic is certainly complex and has not been more than cursorily examined. Of Dutch cakes it can be reported that they are normally iced and decorated with white or pink roses in marzipan. Recently the demand for novelty and extravagance has added further possibilities. Stands which arrange the cakes more elaborately and spectacularly are available in Paris and elsewhere or can be constructed by pâtissiers themselves. Cakes with tiers stacked directly one on top of another ('superposés') have also been possible for a long time (Tante Marie 1954: 142). These may nowadays be based on mousse rather than a cake mixture. Cakes of this kind in the form of buildings, boats or other objects which have a meaning for the couple marrying have also in some places begun to appear. The same Breton pâtissier reported that 30 per cent of his wedding orders were for cakes on stands, 10 per cent for the stacked.

In the French tradition, these cakes are to be admired and enjoyed as high points of the festive wedding meal. In the past they were generally brought in, to acclaim, at the end of the meal. More recently they have typically been kept till late in the evening and their entry has provided a high point for the wedding dance following the meal, to which larger numbers of guests have been invited. Though bride and groom may cut the first pieces, no ritual or ceremony of cutting, distribution or eating has developed. Elsewhere, a development more directly comparable to the British is sometimes to be found. A Dutch tradition is that the groom should cut the first slice for the bride. The bride then cuts for her family, and the staff supporting the occasion for the rest of the company. But in a new age of equality, 'the man and the woman are the same now', said tongue-in-cheek by one pâtissière in the Netherlands. A new pattern of joint cutting was therefore appropriate. In contrast to the British practice, cakes would be cut from the top downwards.

AMERICA

It has been impossible, at least until very recently, to mark any clear boundary between the forms of the cake, its history, uses and meanings west and east of the ocean. Across the Atlantic, contrary traditions from other parts of the European continent were in places assiduously maintained but it was development from the British roots which was, in this as in so many other spheres, most conspicuous. The prehistory of cake-baking and confectionery on which the following chapters focus belongs to the United States as well as to Britain,[1] though there were doubtless corners remote from metropolitan centres where old fashions were maintained and local variants developed. In the nineteenth and earlier twentieth centuries when our cake as a specific institution was formed, the 'black cake', as the plum cake has often been called in America, for long retained its place as the wedding cake *par excellence*. On both sides of the Atlantic it was to a remarkable degree the enterprise and enthusiasm of immigrants from continental Europe, men such as Schülbe, Willy, Hueg and Bauer, who developed the distinctive artefact and contributed to its popularity.

The dominance of the rich fruit cake was, however, less in America. The poundcake, which on the British side of the Atlantic was usually a fruit cake (but see Glasse 1747: 138), was a plain and white cake. Whiteness indeed became a theme of American cake-making as it never did in Britain, with Angel (Food) Cakes as a characteristic development. Recipes were commonly called 'White Cake', providing a sharp contrast with the so-called 'Black Cake'. Poundcakes and white cakes came to be used for festive occasions such as Christmas even in the late eighteenth century (Weaver 1990). There came therefore to be a choice which there never was in Britain between a white and a black cake for weddings. A tendency to specialise terms also appeared: the white cake tended to take on the older designation 'bride's cake' – perhaps, as something light and white, being seen as having more affinity with the bride[2] – whereas the black cake was more likely to be called a wedding cake (e.g. Hueg 1901: 25, 27, 48). The former might have a soft white icing or frosting,[3] the latter a hard (Farmer 1911: 191–3, 199–200). There was, however, never an altogether firm distinction here. Elaborate decoration in similar styles to the British on the outside might disguise the presence of an American white cake on the inside.

Except perhaps in parts of the east with a strong sense of status and tradition, the white alternative gained the upper hand in the twentieth century (e.g. Rombauer & Becker 1973: 623–4). This meant that most American cakes did not follow the British development of tiers elevated on pillars. If more than a single cake were required, the previously established pattern of layers of declining size stacked directly one on another persisted. Since the white cake would bake better in thinner layers than were usual for fruit cakes (ibid.), it was typically a piling up of more but thinner tiers than in the British pattern.

Already in the 1890s, therefore, a choice of cakes had been established in America. The types could be played with, for commercial and/or symbolic effect. One idea was to give the bridegroom a cake to match the bride's, and this might be simply achieved by renaming the rich fruit style. A 'Lady Cake or Plain Bridegroom Cake' for which the recipe was published in *The British Baker* in 1897 as an importation from 'across the herring pond' (Vine 1897: 68; see Rorer 1902: 617) was, however, a white cake. The author explains that it is 'supposed to be cut by the bridegroom and distributed with a glass of wine to the bridesmaids before going to church'. In Britain neither practice nor cake met with any success, but in the United States the two cakes did persist, with the light cake usually being associated with the bride, the dark with the groom. From the mid-century a possible combination of the two has been described from Virginia (Frese 1982). The bride's would be on the bottom. Bride and groom would cut it at the reception, give pieces to each other to eat, and it would be served to the guests. The groom's would be mounted above it and saved for later consumption. Subsequently, it has been claimed, the groom's tended to drop out, as 'the second cake', leaving the bride's to be regarded as the wedding cake. Such cakes might still be entirely white poundcakes flavoured with almond or vanilla, or the bottom layer might be of this mixture with an upper layer or layers of whatever took the fancy of the particular couple. They might choose 'spice, carrot, chocolate chip, or applesauce raisin'. Cutting pieces of cake for one another might on occasion be taken a step further, becoming a jokey game in which the bride, offering her groom the first gooey slice, slams it into his face in a move not entirely remote from the great American custard-pie tradition (Tuleja 1987: 63–4).

By this point, the common Anglo-American roots of the wedding cake were becoming remote. Practices had diverged to a point at which the idiom on one side of the Atlantic might seem distinctly unfamiliar to people on the other. By the 1970s, in Los Angeles at least, cakes were to be seen in an array of fantasy styles, sometimes with ethnic titles or motifs. One firm was offering 'Pure Bridal White, Daring German Chocolate, Classic Italian Marble and Secret Danish Gold'. They claimed that they had 'innovated chocolate wedding cakes in L.A., to keep up with the new freedom of expression', and went on to comment that 'it really upset some people. It's wild what we're doing, but who says it has to be the same old four-tiered white cake year after year?' (Seligson 1974: 100–1). By the 1980s the new freedom had spread more widely. By then, with revival as well as innovation becoming conspicuous, the resources from which these could work were again partly the shared roots. Sometimes cakes recreated the rich fruit and piped ornamentation from the earlier period, sometimes they deserted the piled form, to mingle in typical post-modern style pillars and other elements from past styles, with staircases, bridges and confectionery re-creations of almost any object meaningful to the couple marrying: 'One, a gazebo with latticework, had french doors and a roof decorated with little flower pots. Another was in the shape of a basket decorated with yellow and white flowers. A third consisted of three layers, each one supported by fluted columns. A fourth. . . .'[4]

AUSTRALIA

In Australia, despite its varied immigrant population, the British cake remained dominant but not in any static and unchanging form.[5] The major change which has been noted in the British trade in the 1980s had its roots in an Australian enthusiasm for sugarcraft and cake-decoration which began in the 1950s. This was a period of creativity similar in many ways to the 1890s in Britain which will be examined in Chapter 6. Incongruous as it may seem in the British context, however, in Australia agricultural shows were amongst the formative factors. They provided competition classes for decorated cakes and in this way promoted experimentation. A distinctive new style developed.

This was based on a change of material. Royal icing was demoted from its pre-eminence as the standard material for covering and decorating all the more important cakes to a mere auxiliary for piping. Two other substances to be used in conjunction with it became essential. For covering there was 'plastic icing', a cold-mixed alternative to cooked fondant icing, made with glucose, gelatine, glycerine and flavouring, in addition to icing sugar and water. For modelling it was a version of the ancient sugarpaste, to be discussed in Chapter 6, made with gum tragacanth. In *The Australian Book of Cake Decorating* (1973), Bernice Vercoe, one of the leaders of the movement from the 1950s onwards, wrote: 'We do not recommend royal icing for coverings as this mixture is hard and brittle when dry and tends to crack and separate from the cake when cut', but 'the English still use it'. 'In Australia royal icing is used for pipework only.' Plastic icing, on the other hand, 'remains soft to the bite for long and indefinite periods' (Vercoe 1976: 10–11). It is also easier to use, being rolled out and draped and conformed to almost any shape; it does not have to be smoothed on moist and allowed to set. The very considerable skill needed to achieve a fine, smooth surface even on regular shapes with royal icing becomes redundant.

Using these materials all sorts of novelty modelling and effects were possible, but there quickly developed a formal style as distinctive as the one it was replacing. The fruit-cake base and the scheme of tiering survived, but the decorative scheme was revolutionised. Instead of a sharp top edge to each cake, made a focus for decoration, the new style offered a more or less rounded edge and a flat top left free of surface decoration. The emphasis shifted to this flat top and to the base of the sides. Around these latter a variety of delicate fringes of piped extension work would be created. The conception underlying all these designs was of a soft tablecloth laid over the cake, fringed and then decorated on the surface, mainly its lower portions, with delicate patterns of 'embroidery'. The top surfaces were undecorated, except for the occasional little motif such as a tiny bluebird, but provided platforms for the display of delicately modelled and coloured sugarpaste flowers. These were often of spectacular beauty and were the leading, and very costly, feature of such cakes. The total effect was soft and rounded, making a virtue of characteristics which were not present in the hard, crisply decorated, upstanding British cake. It seems to be directed to the likely taste of a bride in a way that the British has never been. Vercoe (1976: 108) describes a stacked cake – another similar is described as 'an American Beauty' – as 'popular with brides who like to get away from the separated tiered look. Softly feminine in appearance, yet simple in design. . . .'

The books which described and illustrated these cakes so lavishly were often republished in Britain. In this way Australian ideas could become widely known, with the implications for the trade and for the wedding cake itself which have already been touched on and which will be examined further below.

OUTWITH THE WEST

Wedding cakes of one or other of these kinds, or developments from them, were then carried to countries of European settlement where they might also be taken up by indigenous peoples persuaded of the superiority of Euro-American practices. In the era of extensive western technological and cultural dominance, strongly supported by expansion of mass media in the second half of the twentieth century, wedding cakes were taken up even more widely.

Monica Wilson (1972; cf. Hunter 1936: 217) used the cake as a focus for explicit discussion of cultural change in the South African context. Her account of Nguni African practice is tantalisingly brief but it reaches back to the 1930s, revealing two cakes of basically British type but differentiated by the colour of their icing. A white three-tier cake would be provided by the bride's side and a blue one by the groom's. The two would be paraded and danced around in competitive spirit. Both would be cut by the bride. This was to observe local White practice, even to take advice from local Europeans on doing it properly, but at the same time it departed creatively from its models in response to the characteristic relationship between the two sides in Nguni marriages.[6]

In southern India the British connection likewise installed a cake of British style, taken up amongst Christians in Kerala and elsewhere. In the 1980s one firm in the city of Bangalore produced tiered and pillared wedding cakes for a local Catholic population, topped by a miniature bride and groom. Here the fruit-cake centre had proved too costly and had therefore been replaced by a dummy to be hired. Cutting remained important however. A wedge of fruit cake was therefore included in the base to provide something into which it was possible actually to cut. The sugar icing was entirely real and intended to be taken off, distributed and eaten.

By the 1980s experimentation following pictures of American cakes and a booming trade in original birthday cakes were leading away from the standard white three tiers and pillars, in the direction of more representational cakes. As elsewhere the possibility of placing the tiers differently in relation to one another had been seen: three might for instance be mounted at different heights and linked by sugarpaste steps and bridges. They then provided a romantic monument for bride and groom, in imagination, to climb together. Commoner were sponge cakes for weddings, usually just oblong or round, but occasionally mounted too, using pillars for a second tier cut through the soft bottom one to the solid base. The market in Bangalore was tending to decrease. Here as elsewhere it was solely Christian; the majority Hindu population had their own vigorous and very different traditions both of wedding celebration and of catering.

Egypt provided an interesting parallel but here the favoured imperial link was with France and the cake, again probably used by the Christian population, was a creamy gâteau of continental European style. In the 1980s small plaster bride-and-groom figures were widely available to be set atop such cakes.

Japan shows in particularly spectacular form the way in which contemporary western patterns could spread fast around the world in the postwar period of mass communications. Edwards (1984) writes: 'Wedding cakes first appeared in the lavish and highly publicized weddings of celebrities in the postwar period, and were later adopted by ordinary persons. Hakutsruden [the marriage hall he studied in 1982–83] began offering wedding cakes to its customers in 1970.'[7] At first they were real cakes, cut and served, but these were too expensive for demand to develop satisfactorily. 'The cake, and the ceremony that began to develop around it, became more popular after the introduction of artificial cakes reduced the cost to Y8,000 in 1973.' And in a few years the new style attained an almost universal popularity: 95.5 per cent of 228 receptions at the hall took it.

> The outward appearance of the cake is borrowed directly from Western tradition. It is the white bride's cake in its most elaborate form, with three and sometimes four tiers and nearly four feet high, topped by miniature figures of a bridal couple in Western dress. Long red and white ribbons stream from their feet down to the base of the cake.

But the cake is inedible and even the elaborate 'icing' is hard wax or, as a recent innovation, moulded rubber. A decorated knife has to be thrust into the 'cake' by bride and groom together, and for this a slot is provided at the back. The whole thing indeed exists for this insertion and for the standard photograph to be taken at that time. A mechanism may respond to the thrusting in of the knife with a dramatic cloud of steam. The story Edwards tells here is of a rapid build up of ritual around the 'cake', with commercial advantage as its powerful engine.

THEMES

The British wedding cake is therefore distinctive, but a more general Euro-American cultural form of which it is a localised manifestation is clearly recognisable. The wedding cake, besides acknowledging the culturally specific idea that a cake should be a part of marriage celebration, has had two striking characteristics. The first and most obvious is its tendency to rise in tiers of decreasing size. The common grounding here is the desire to rise high and be impressive, but exactly how this is to be achieved has varied according to the different local culinary and festive traditions within which it has been attempted. The British tradition which we shall be examining in subsequent chapters grew, partly directly and partly by revival from continental models, out of elements developed originally in late medieval times and early modern times. The continental traditions were, in contrast, formed within the later developing and in a sense more sophisticated world of the specialised pâtissier. The distinctive American forms are then different again, having emerged out of the already specialised British tradition by innovation and adaptation within a different and culturally less homogeneous society.

The second characteristic, negative but highlighted by recent developments, has been for such confections to hold back from the figurative. Unlike medieval subtleties or modern 'novelties' they have not until recently imitated other objects but have established forms of their own. These have been susceptible to many variations, but always have been immediately recognisable as wedding cakes. In their decoration a strong tendency towards the abstract has everywhere been apparent. These characteristics seem probably to relate to the nature of western marriage and the values surrounding it. This will be discussed later. Changes in the forms of cakes and their presentation which were finally becoming conspicuous almost everywhere during the 1980s may well mark a turning point in the institution of marriage in these societies (Charsley 1991).

3 Cultural creation
Myth, history and language

THE VICTORIAN MYTH OF ORIGIN

The degree to which the wedding cake and the uses to which it is put in twentieth century Britain have become standardised may well mislead when the past is considered. Even the degree of standardisation already present in the later nineteenth century misled J. C. Jeaffreson whose *Brides and Bridals* (1872) offered a pioneering account of the history of the cake. Other writers have subsequently followed him, sometimes themselves adding to the confusion by misinterpreting his words in terms of the cakes with which they were familiar in their own day (e.g. Charsley 1988). This is surely a way in which history can properly be distinguished from myth if the will to do so is there. Myth looks to the past to explain whatever is perceived to be important in the present; history seeks, like the anthropologist in another country, to understand the differentness of the past on its own terms. These are different enterprises in so far as anyone wishes to make them so. History, to the extent that it impinges at all on anyone's present, contextualises it rather than explaining why it should be so.

Jeaffreson's 'history' is in these terms an interesting example of the myth-making of its period. Like others then, before, and even since (Baker 1977: 111), he was led by a sense that, to be properly grounded, contemporary practice must have a lineage going back to ancient Rome. This was to make a link with the region of history so special for the identity of European societies as they developed out of the middle ages as to be labelled 'classical'. At times and amongst people aware of their own imperial status, such links were at a premium. Classical practice, like the Latin language, despite all its historical diversity, could seem a bedrock on which the present had to be founded. The story Jeaffreson told began, therefore, with an ancient Roman marriage practice involving the breaking of a 'cake' over the bride's head. It jumped to evidence from the England of a thousand and more years later, for the pouring or throwing of grain, and from this to supposed survivals around Britain as late as his own century of the breaking of biscuit, 'cake' or 'bread' over the bride.

The problem was then to discover a continuous chain coming forward in time to the elaborate cakes familiar amongst the more prosperous classes of his own day. It could apparently be accomplished via a comment by a distinguished antiquarian and observer of the seventeenth century, John Aubrey (1626–97) – though Jeaffreson actually confused him with John Evelyn, the diarist and authority on horticulture and forestry. Aubrey comments in his *The Remaines of Gentilisme and Judaisme* (1686–7/1881) on a change of custom between the time of his boyhood and his adult life. As a boy before the Civil War in England he remembered attending a wedding feast and seeing cakes piled up on the table. The bride and groom would kiss over the cakes.[1] It was, Jeaffreson considered, with the arrival in England of French confectionery skills and influences at the Restoration in 1660 that the pile of cakes was consolidated with an overall covering of icing and decoration. This pile could still be broken over the bride's head; the small individual cakes would fall out. It was, however, well on the way to the modern English wedding cake of his day. He writes:

> A section of a properly composed bridal-cake displays indications of what may be termed the historical development of our grandest piece of confectionery. The layers of almond paste, which divide the plum-work, are regarded by the philosophical antiquary less as material for the enrichment of the composition than as memorials of the time when the wedding-cake consisted of several cakes, each of which had its coating of almond sweetmeat or sugar-ice.
>
> (Jeaffreson 1872: 289)

There is no doubt that this story is fanciful and wrong, though its subsequent repetition shows that he had created a myth which would appear appropriate to those few who have thought to question the cake's origins. It is wrong in basing itself on his own historically uninformed perception of the cake with which he was familiar, a form which was in some respects exceptionally transitory, as will be seen. It is wrong in treating this as a unitary thing, a single indivisible whole which must therefore have a single origin. If these errors can be avoided – and it is always surprisingly difficult to do so – the evidence exists from which to construct a much more adequate account of the development of the wedding cake. Its forerunners before Jeaffreson's period can be examined and the story continued over the century and more which has passed since he was writing.

CULTURAL HISTORY AND ITS PROBLEMS

In such an enquiry, variability has constantly to be kept in mind. Van Gennep's magnificent compendium of French custom, *Du Berceau à la Tombe (Manuel de Folklore Français Contemporain)* (1946), documents the immense variability of custom in rural France, from region to region, district to district, often village to village, in the period before the homogenising processes of the twentieth century took hold. Even if Britain's regional cultures weakened rather earlier (Brears 1987: 188) and were perhaps never so markedly various, and even if the record of them is, for a number of reasons, weaker than the French, it must be assumed that the evidence which is available represents no more than sporadic traces of particular local practices. Indeed, customs which are unfamiliar to an observer, or are expected to be unfamiliar to the audience to whom the observer will report, are more likely to be recorded than those which appear ordinary, even natural. Van Gennep repeatedly notes the problem of dealing with this standard warping of the available evidence.

Similar comments have to be made about the passage of time and about differences related to class, status and wealth. A dominant class often sees its practice as standing for the whole. It may indeed succeed in making its practices the model to which others aspire. Jeaffreson's modern English wedding cake was coming to be characteristic of his class in the second half of the nineteenth century, but it was certainly not general in the population at large. It was financially beyond the reach of most people and there is no evidence of any general aspiration towards it at the time. But even a particular locality or a particular class cannot be assumed to have held constantly to practices known to be associated with it at one time or place, or the practices to have evolved according to any standard pattern. Van Gennep stresses local inventiveness. The power of example should be added to this. A successful celebration becomes a model to be followed by others who attend or hear about it. Fashions come and go. Like Mr Selby in Richardson's *Sir Charles Grandison* (1753–4), people may revive customs of their youth, in that instance the bridegroom waiting at table at the bridal banquet. However each individual event works out, it becomes inevitably a part of the experience of those who have participated in it. It moulds both their understanding of 'tradition' and their subsequent aspirations as and when they themselves assume control of a similar kind of event. There is therefore in principle not one story to be told for Britain or even England, but multiple local stories. Most of these are entirely unreachable. A level of generalising is therefore as inevitable as it is proper, but it is important not to lose sight of the nature of this process.

The important initial step is to break down the sense that the familiar culturally created object – for this study the late twentieth century British wedding cake – is a single inevitable entity. Such objects are always likely to be a cluster of features or components with distinct histories. In the case of the cake the feature which has the longest history and shows most continuity is the mixture from which it is made. The way it is iced and decorated is another with its own distinctive history, and its shape and the uses to which it is put are two more. Such features are held together, at every moment and through time too, by the terms by which they are collectively identified. An understanding of these separate aspects of the wedding cake's history provides a far more secure basis than has previously been available for examining meanings as they have been and may be attached to it.

RECIPES AS EVIDENCE

As ephemeral, everyday cultural creations, food objects in European traditions are more accessible to long-term study than most. In an increasingly literate culture written records of the ways in which particular dishes had been and should be prepared began to seem useful in the later middle ages. There is no reason to imagine any single situation as having given rise to them and it is difficult to know in the earlier periods who would have written them and who exactly would have been intended to read them (Henisch 1976: 144–5). Nevertheless, their general characteristics are clear. They were from the beginning immediately practical instructions, apparently directed to those familiar with the processes of cookery and their ingredients. There was much therefore that was not explained or specified. The most famous British example is *The Forme of Cury*, an early manuscript of which makes the plausible claim that it was compiled by the master cooks of King Richard II of England, with the help of the masters of 'phisik and of philosophie that dwellid in his court'. This would date it from about 1390. Its stated object was to teach the making of 'commune' and 'curious' dishes, at least the former 'craftly and holsomely' (Hieatt & Butler 1985: 20 and *passim*). Records of practice within great households such as this, perhaps as reference works for those directing the preparation of food for royal and noble tables and for feasts, were always prominent. Individual recipes and collections were often much copied.

With the development of printing there emerged an almost entirely new possibility, of writing and producing books which would, as a commercial product, sell more widely and to less relevantly informed readers. Thenceforth the range of types of book which might contain recipes changed and evolved. In general, earlier books of revelation led on to books of instruction, and the instructions became ever more exact and comprehensive. As material which might be included accumulated and publications typically fed on their predecessors, they became more specialised.

Cakes, subtleties, marchpanes and icing – the items which will chiefly concern us in the following chapters – belonged initially in the realm of 'mysteries' or 'secrets'. The offer of revelation was at first a major selling point, exploited by numerous publishers and authors. The assemblage of secrets was often diverse. Cures for the ills of old age and a host of specific ailments might be juxtaposed with beauty treatments, cooking recipes and household hints for improving the quality of life in a variety of ways, for removing stains, making alcoholic drinks, preserving fruit and making ornaments of sugarpaste. Such works in time gave rise to more specialised books, the primary attraction of which was however still revelatory. Those on cookery, bakery and confectionery are of most direct interest here. In them were collected recipes used in great houses in order to display them to a wider circle. A profusion of recipes came soon to be offered, typically compiled with little system and differing from one another mainly in the person or place from which they originated. But in the eighteenth century revelation began to transmute into instruction. What the reader might need to know in order to be able to follow instructions was increasingly considered, and systematic ways of presenting the material were developed. Lists of ingredients clearly specified as to weights, and exact instructions as to how they were to be handled and combined, became the standard form. The cookbook became, indeed, the proverbial exemplar of explicit instruction.

Instruction might be intended for more or less specialised readerships. Nutt (1809) wrote for 'OPULENT FAMILIES, both in town and country, who wish to give handsome OCCASIONAL entertainments to their select friends; and who, on such occasions, are not so scrupulous of expense'. In the later eighteenth and nineteenth centuries, cookery, baking and confectionery were often located within a general handbook for those running households. These might be assumed to be grand or more modest, and books were occasionally aimed explicitly at one or the other. The newly married, in charge of a household for the first time, were an obvious market and, in works aimed at them, everything might need to be explained. A line of such works, often published and republished over long periods, reached its apotheosis in 'Mrs Beeton', the instructional equivalent of the bulky Victorian novel, which first appeared in book form in 1861.

Instruction might also be directed to one or other of the trades involved, to cooks, bakers or confectioners producing for retail sale, or to the catering trade in restaurants and hotels. Books might record current practice, either at large or in some particular establishment, or they might propagate novelties. The extent to which they claimed originality varied greatly. Copyright law, in principle since 1711 but in practice increasingly in recent times, introduced an acute pressure on subsequent authors to vary the recipes of their predecessors. A growing exactness in the specification of ingredients and their weights had the incidental effect of dealing with any difficulty here. Since minor variations in proportions are important only occasionally for the results achieved, plenty of details to be varied were often available. Novelties were not infrequently imported and were sometimes so extensive as to be characterised as an entire nouvelle cuisine. Authors' theories about healthy or otherwise appropriate food likewise sometimes featured in forewords or in interpolated comments. Many works included elements of several of these different possibilities.

When it comes to using recipes from these sources as evidence there are obvious problems. It has sometimes been said that cookery books reflect the practice of the preceding generation. Given their very varied background this is obviously an oversimplification, though it may be a fair judgement on many a pedestrian work taken as a whole. Some published recipes represent, indeed, proposals which few people will subsequently even have tried, let alone have adopted. Some, for one reason or another, are incorrect or impracticable. Others may have been old at the time of their first publication, but were by means of it spread far more widely. What can be inferred from a published recipe is therefore limited. One fact is always indisputable however: it did exist at a particular date, if only on the printed page. The history of the publication of recipes, while not the same thing as the history of dishes being consumed even amongst the book-buying classes, does therefore provide a basis for an account of trends and their approximate dating. Of particular value is the positive evidence provided by new editions. In general it is striking how recipes in popular books have been repeated with little change over long periods; changes are telling therefore. When they are made they suggest strongly either that something previously acceptable has ceased to be so and now needs to be replaced, or that something which did not seem necessary before now needs to be included. The evidential value of a recipe at its first appearance is therefore considerable; its subsequent publication unchanged has very little significance. Such evidence has always therefore to be used carefully, but it has the enormous advantage of relative profusion.

Documentary evidence of other kinds, though it is often scarce for so taken-for-granted an aspect of life, provides an important supplement to the recipes whenever it is available.

'WEDDING CAKE' AND 'BRIDE CAKE': TERMS IN LANGUAGE

The term 'wedding cake' could have been used at any time, whenever a cake had any prominent place in wedding celebrations. A poem by Robert Herrick provides evidence that this was so as early as the first half of the seventeenth century. The poem, published in *Hesperides* in 1648 but possibly written as much as a generation earlier, deserves quoting in full:

The Bride-cake

This day my *Julia* thou must make
For Mistresse Bride, the wedding Cake:
Knead but the Dow and it will be
To paste of Almonds turn'd by thee:
Or kisse it thou, but once, or twice,
And for the Bride-Cake ther'l be Spice.

This is one of a set of love poems to Julia and has to be understood in that light (Shawcross 1978). Though it may seem to have been designed explicitly to tempt subsequent readers into anachronistic interpretation, it does, as will be seen in Chapter 6, provide important evidence for more than terms.

The same poem, other poems in the same collection, and other early references make it clear that the usual term was 'bride cake' (Aubrey 1881: 139). The term is recorded by lexicographers from the middle of the preceding century (Huloet 1552; Baret 1580) and it was one of a set of forms at the period, all emphasising the focal position of the bride. Only 'bridesmaid' remains today entirely unchallenged, though even it has long had a partial alternative in Scotland in the term 'best maid'. 'Bridegroom' is now routinely shortened to 'groom', a form which avoids the historic focus on the bride and more easily allows a conception of equivalence for the female and male roles. 'Bridal' or 'bride-ale', a term for the festivities themselves, 'bride-laces', 'bride-cup' and 'bride-bed' have gone entirely. In most of these forms 'bridal' and 'bride's' were then and remained possible variants: Herrick's introduction to *Hesperides*, explaining his concerns, includes the lines:

I sing of May-poles, Hock-carts, Wassails, Wakes,
Of Bride-grooms, Brides, and of their Bridall-cakes.

As applied to cakes these forms survived unchallenged until the middle of the nineteenth century. Since that time they have remained as alternatives, merely declining in frequency. In Scotland at least they were still to be encountered in the 1980s, suggesting perhaps a rather more tenacious link there to the bride herself.

Mrs Beeton and her publications mark the transition, though belatedly (cf. Dickens 1846/1971: 34). The book which established her fame, *The Book of Household Management*, offered a recipe for 'Rich Bride or Christening Cake' (Beeton 1861: 854). When she came, however, a few pages later to discuss the catering more generally, she referred to its centrepiece as a 'wedding cake'. She offered a 'bill of fare for a Ball Supper, or a Cold Collation for a Summer Entertainment, or Wedding or Christening Breakfast for 70 or 80 Persons' (Beeton 1861: 858). If it was to be a wedding breakfast, it was the presence of the cake which would distinguish it as such. For a time the two terms could suggest some difference of meaning: at the Universal Cookery and Food Exhibition held in London in 1888, the competition class for large, elaborate and hugely expensive cakes described them as 'wedding cakes', in contrast to another class for 'two-guinea *bride-cakes*'. Jeaffreson too was probably thinking of the grander items when he titled his chapter 'Wedding-cake'. Mrs Beeton, however, when she came to publish her more popular and cheaper *Every-day Cookery and Housekeeping Book* in 1872, the same year as Jeaffreson's book, retitled her recipe 'Rich Wedding-cake'. This major change was therefore in the process of establishing itself, aided in some measure, however slight, by Jeaffreson himself, at the same time as he was dwelling on the traditional nature of the institution. There is a lesson in this.

4   When the wedding cake was not yet and might never have been

FEASTS, FOODS AND SUBTLETIES

In the medieval period neither cakes in the usual modern sense nor icing had yet appeared.[1] Nothing directly equivalent to the wedding cake could therefore have any part in the celebration of marriages. Feasts and celebrations might be held but marriage was simply their occasion. No specialised food object had a place at them, nor was there as far as has been recorded any special action of a ritual nature using any food item as part of the wedding. Medieval feasting is nevertheless one of the roots from which cakes and their use in weddings were to grow. This should be discussed first since it is what contributed most directly to the material basis of the cake. It is the church ritual of marriage which was the basis for its use.

Decoratively presented foods and those using imported ingredients of high cost were features of medieval feasting. Dishes, often combining both, were developed in the highest reaches of society where the wealth for their creation was available and display was an important prop to status and power. The recipe for blank maunger from *The Forme of Cury*, a collection from about 1390 discussed in the previous chapter, epitomises such cooking with its almonds and rice ('rys') and sugar, and its concern for colour:

> Take capouns and seeth hem, thenne take hem up; take almaundes blaunched. Grynde hem & alay [mix] hem up with the same broth. Cast the mylk in a pot. Waisshe rys and do [put] therto, and lat it seeth; thanne take the brawn of the capouns, teere it small and do [put] therto. Take white grece, sugur and salt, and cast therinne. Lat it seeth; thenne messe it forth and florissh it with aneys in confyt, rede other whyt [i.e. garnish it with aniseed coated in red and white sugar], and with almaundes fryed in oyle, and serve it forth.
>
> (Hieatt & Butler 1985: 106, 151)

As a determinedly white dish this already has a certain relevance to the whiteness of iced cakes three hundred years in the future. It is, however, dark festive ingredients which are more directly relevant. 'Plumb' or 'plum' was to be the key term here. It represents a family of festive foods to which it became attached in the sixteenth century. From then on, 'plum' dishes in various guises proliferated and spread widely through society. They still have their descendants in modern British cooking, of which the wedding cake is one. Plum potage, plum porridge, plum broth, plum cake, plum pie, plum pudding, plum buns and plum duff are its historic forms. The 'plum' in all of these stands for dried fruit, raisins – sometimes termed 'of the sun' – raisins of Corinth or currants, raisins of the sun – which became simply 'raisins' – and occasionally others. Such dried and imported fruit, imported spice and, in the earlier dishes, meat are the key ingredients. Cinnamon, nutmeg and mace were the spices most commonly used. Several such dishes have at various times been associated with Christmas and to a lesser extent with other festive occasions. The cost of their ingredients always ensured that for most people they could at best only be special-occasion foods, distinguished as sweet and rich and suitable for treats. Their still vigorous descendants, besides the wedding cake, are the Christmas pudding and cake, mince pies, black or Scotch bun, hot-cross-buns and Simnel cake.

The plum pie has the most intricate and interesting history. Early recipes combining meat, dried fruit and spices, with a variety of other ingredients, are not uncommon, and *The Forme of Cury* has a rather direct forerunner in its recipe for Tartletes (Hieatt & Butler 1985: 137–8, 218). In modern English it would read:

> Take boiled veal and grind it small. Take hard-boiled eggs and grind them, and add whole prunes, dates cut up, pine-kernels, currants, whole spices and powdered spices, sugar and salt; and make a little pie-case and put the mixture in. Cover it and bake it and serve it out.

By the early seventeenth century this kind of recipe might appear as a 'Christmas pie' or a 'mince('d) pie', as Robert Herrick's 'Ceremonies for Christmasse' bears witness:

> Drink now the strong Beere,
> Cut the white loafe here,
> The while the meat is a shredding
> For the rare Mince-Pie;
> To fill the Paste that's a kneading.

A recipe using neat's, i.e. bullock's, tongue was published in *The Compleat Cook* in 1655. In Scotland such celebrations were registered as distinctively English (Halkett 1979: 69). Essentially the same dish remained popular into the nineteenth century, only then being gradually transformed by the loss of its meat to the familiar modern dish.

These meat-and-sweet 'plum' dishes had been English classics, fit for celebration. *The Oxford English Dictionary* (*OED*) cites a mock sermon from some time before 1660 discoursing on the variety of plum pies: 'He that discovered the new Star in Cassiopeia . . . deserves not half so much to be remembered as he that first married minced meat and Raisins together.' The subsequent loss of the meat catches the sea-change that has come over British eating in the centuries since. The modern structures of meals around the day, of courses within meals, of dishes within courses, and of ingredients in dishes crept in only gradually and piecemeal. A key opposition in the new order was between sweet and savoury; 'meat' itself had been a general term in medieval English, not yet specialised to the flesh of animals. The very concept of 'savoury' in opposition to sweet had to be created for this to be possible; its first use in such a sense recorded in the *OED* comes from as late as 1661. Savouries came to be separate from and generally to precede sweets. With ideas structured in terms of this opposition, the plum dishes came to seem distinctly anomalous. Elaborate meals of the past, even those as recent as the ones described by Mrs Beeton in the mid-nineteenth century, would appear to the puzzled understanding of a later age no more than jumbles of discordant foods.

The plum cake, however, was unusual. Never having contained meat, it could survive without radical change into the new order. Particularly in its wedding-cake form, this mixture is therefore a survivor. It could well symbolise in the present a long and distinctively British – and before that English – tradition of celebratory eating.

Festive ingredients, in particular almonds, dried fruit, sugar and spices, are one relevant legacy; display is another which again took off in the highest circles as the middle ages came to an end. From the late fourteenth century, 'soteltes', or subtleties, are prominent in records of feasting. Sutton & Hammond (1983: 383) write, of medieval banquets, 'The mood of display, self-congratulation, aspiration and gentle propaganda was typified in the subtleties, elaborate confections of sugar, pastry, wax, paint and paper, the ancestors of the modern wedding cake and the pride of the master cook' (cf. Henisch 1976: 228–34). This is well exemplified in a document of such relevance to present concerns that it has to be set out in some detail. 'Ffor to make a feast for a bryde' is a section of *Ffor to Serve a Lord*, an instructional work in English dated to around 1500 (Furnivall 1868: 349–60). It offers a prescription for a late medieval wedding feast amongst the aristocracy.[2]

The first course[3] as described begins with brawn, accompanied by 'the' boar's head lying in a field. There is writing round about it, a verse of welcome to the guests and good wishes addressed particularly to the bride. A series of other dishes are then listed for this course, before the description ends with a 'sotelte': 'A lambe stondyng in scriptour, saying on this wyse: "I meekly unto you, sovrayne, am sente, to dwell with you and ever be present." ' The description of the second course begins with venison in broth and 'viaunde Ryalle', a spiced blancmange-like sweet, thickened with rice flour (Hieatt & Butler 1985: 120). After several other dishes the prescription ends again with a subtlety: 'An antelope sayng[4] on a sele that saith with scriptour "beith all gladd & mery that sitteth at this messe, and prayeth for the king and all his".' The third course starts with cream of almonds and lozenge in syrup. It then has a number of other dishes which include three fish described as 'in sotelte' – perhaps set up as if alive (cf. Hieatt & Butler 1985: 215) – and finally 'a bake mete with a sotelte: an angell with a scriptour, "thank all, god, of this feste" '.

The fourth course is clearly different. It does not have the range of meats and sweets of the others, but it is difficult to know exactly what is indicated: 'Payne puff, chese, freynes, brede hote, with a cake, and a wif lying in childe-bed, with a scriptour saing in this wyse, "I am comyng toward your bryde. yf ye dirste onys loke to me ward, I wene ye nedys muste." ' There follows 'another course or servise' but it seems to be no more than a final snack since it lacks both any elaborately made dish and any subtlety.

Payne puff here is a possible forerunner of the plum cake, a meat-and-sweet dish but made, in the *Forme of Cury* recipe, with bone marrow (Hieatt & Butler 1985: 204). It is difficult to know what 'a cake' here represents (see the following section) but their significance has perhaps to be read in the context of a course, the subtlety for which makes an explicit link to birth and the bride. It is possible even that a great cake from the bridal procession was intended. The 'scriptour' on this subtlety is puzzling and perhaps intentionally ambiguous. Is the 'I' who is coming a baby, childbirth or even the bed? Henisch (1976: 232–3) interprets this as meaning: 'if you dare glance in my direction once I think you must (conceive a child)'. She writes: 'Half the fun of the "wif-lying in childe-bed" sotelty would have been lost if teasing guests and blushing, brand-new bride and groom had been allowed to overlook its mock-sinister "scriptour".'

Subtleties were therefore a feature of grand eating in the late medieval period. They were produced with considerable ingenuity and sometimes artistry, and they might have motifs related to the particular occasion of the feast: distinctively wedding subtleties were therefore, as here, a possibility, but there is no evidence that any standard form ever developed and most of the wedding feasts recorded lack them altogether. They were not specifically English. Indeed they certainly developed earlier and were taken to more sophisticated heights at the courts of kings and great lords of the European mainland (Vanaise 1928: 9–11). Unlike the plum tradition, the pedigree which links subtleties to the efflorescence of the wedding cake in the nineteenth century is neither direct and continuous nor specifically English. We must await Chapter 7 before taking it further.

CAKE, GREAT CAKES AND MARRIAGE RITES

'Cake' as a term appears but rarely in early recipes and never as the name of a dish. Its presence in the wedding feast above is therefore surprising. Even today as a term it retains a variety of meanings and usages and all that can be certain about that cake is that it was not one in the primary modern sense. This, in culinary contexts, makes it one of the basic categories by which thinking about food and its types is structured. It has come to stand for sweet, flour-based, baked food, contrasting with 'bread' which stands for flour-based, baked food without (noticeable) sweetening. Bread is normally raised by yeast, cake in other ways. This is not to say that the range of food actually produced fits easily into such a division, but when items do not the basic terms are qualified: there are various kinds of sweet 'breads' some of which, like shortbread, may now seem to be 'not really bread at all' (cf. short*cake* biscuits); boiled cakes and yeast cakes are possibilities, and oatcakes are a clear reminder of a different past. The English medieval cookery books do not contain recipes for cake as such, though the term does appear, unusually, in a recipe for making Bryndons in a book dated to about 1420 (Austin 1888: 15). For this dish 'cakys' are to be made of flour, saffron, sugar, and 'Faire Water'. They are to be made thin, cut in long strips and fried in oil, before being served in a syrup of honey, wine, spice, dates, raisins, etc. Despite the inclusion of sugar here, there is no reason to think that it was the sweetening here which made this a cake. If there is any single ancestral meaning of the term, it seems likely to refer simply to a mouldable plastic substance made by adding moisture to ground grain, or to the object, e.g. an oatcake, made out of it. This might, if baked, also qualify to be termed 'bread'. There is however no evidence of a time at which 'cakes' have not been a heterogeneous lot. The cake of soap should not be forgotten.

What is clear is that the expectations by means of which we

understand the term when we encounter it today are largely the result of developments which have occurred progressively, particularly since the sixteenth century but with increasing speed in recent times. These have included the rise of sugar in the diet (Mintz 1985), and the development of techniques of baking (Wilson 1973: 240–1, 269). The recording of recipes, seeking them out, adapting them and then spreading them, encouraged by printing, have made culinary ideas of ever-increasing variety and complexity available, and the development of specialised commercial cake-making has contributed to this striking development through the experimentation it has engendered. This process is exemplified in the following sections. Here it may just be noted that, in Britain, the stock has not only been enriched indigenously but has benefited from repeated importations, most notably of the very different French tradition of the gâteau based on egg and sugar foam (Wheaton 1983: 177). 'Cake' has not lost its variety of meanings through such developments, but it has become in addition a generic term, a section heading in cookery books and indeed the title for specialised collections of recipes offering a bewildering profusion of differently named varieties of cake. Amongst these is the wedding cake.

What is therefore important to remember when it comes to evaluating evidence from the past is that the term 'cake' carries for us not only a heavy load of its own specialised connotations but also the expectations which go with its generic and structuring sense. Unless a conscious effort is made to strip these away, the past tends constantly to appear more like the present than there is warrant for believing it to have been. This is a problem which recurs throughout the investigation of past cultural forms, but a start can be made in tackling it by concentrating on two basic points: cakes encountered in records from the past cannot be assumed to be either sweetened or baked in an oven.

A seventeenth-century example, useful for other purposes too, may be quoted. It is provided by Dr White Kennet (1660–1728), a distinguished academic and divine who took over an earlier collection of *Remaines* compiled by John Aubrey. As one of his own substantial additions, probably in the last years of the seventeenth century, he reported that

> The maids of Oxfordshire have a way of foreseeing their sweethearts by making a *dumb cake*; that is, on some Fryday-night, several Maids and Batchelors bring every one a littel flower, and every one a littel salt, and every one blows an egge, and every one helps to make it into past [= pastry], then every one makes y^e cake and lays it on the gridiron,[5] and every one turns it, and when bakt enough every one

breaks a piece, and eats one part and laies the other part under their pillow to dream on y^e person they shall marry. But all this to be done in serious silence w'hout one word or one smile, or els the cake looses the name and the vertue.

(Aubrey 1881: 65; cf. Oliver 1832: 493–4)

Aubrey had himself in several places remarked on the occasions around the year for which cakes were used – 'still', he usually adds, since he was convinced that the Civil War and its gunpowder had blown away most of the customs of old England. There were cakes at Twelvetide, i.e. at the end of the Christmas season of festivity – Ben Jonson calls this 'Baby-Cake' in *Christmas his Masque* (1616) – at Easter, at Whitsuntide, and at Home-harvests, i.e. the completion of the bringing in of the harvest. There were also cakes at christenings, weddings and funerals (Jonson 1616: 65, 139). Whether they were sweetened or differentiated in their ingredients for the different seasons and events remains unknown.

As far as the weddings are concerned, one of the roots of their association with 'cakes' was religious, though this was rather thoroughly hidden from succeeding generations by the Reformation of the sixteenth century. Previously, bread would often be blessed at the end of Sunday Mass and distributed. Service books such as the Scottish *Rathen Manual* in the Sarum tradition, dating from the later fifteenth century, included forms for such blessing. Its editor comments: 'To the present day in many parts of Christendom, those who consider themselves unfit to communicate eagerly partake of a special kind of cake or bun that is handed round' (McGregor 1905: 33; cf. McMillan 1931–2: 26). In the Nuptial Mass this usual practice was then somewhat further developed:

After mass there shall be blessed some bread and wine or any pleasant drink in a vessel, and they shall taste it in the name of the Lord:

'Bless O Lord this bread and this drink as Thou didst bless the five loaves in the desert and the six water pots in Cana of Galilee,[6] that all who taste thereof may be healthy, sober, and undefiled.'

(McGregor 1905: 41)

Evidence for the way customs related to such practices might extend beyond the church walls is scarce but what there is points towards processions. From the end of the sixteenth century comes an account of a wedding supposed to have taken place in or shortly before 1513. This is from Thomas Deloney's *The Pleasant History of John Winchcombe*. Winchcombe, alias Jack of Newbury, was a successful and wealthy Berkshire clothier. His bride's procession to church is described:

Then there was a fair Bride-cup of silver and gilt carried before her, wherein was a goodly branch of Rosemary gilded very faire, hung about with silken Ribands of all colours; next was there a noyse of Musicians that played all the way before her; after her came all the chiefest maydens of the Country, some bearing great Bride Cakes, and some Garlands of wheate finely gilded, and so she past unto the Church.

(Deloney 1912: 22)

The abolition of such blessings at the Reformation, and the abandonment of the Nuptial Mass, must be presumed to have undermined any such procedure. Cakes and cup might still feature in wedding celebrations but cut away from their previous moorings in regular religious practice. Robert Laneham records the entertainments provided for Queen Elizabeth I on a visit to Kenilworth Castle in 1575. These included a mock 'country bride-ale'. In the procession for this were three 'prety puzels [= *pucelles* = maidens] . . . that carried three speciall spisecakes of a bushell of wheat, (they had it by meazure oout of my Lord's bakehouse), before the Bryde . . .' (Laneham 1907: 23). Dekker's play *Satiro-mastix* (1602) supports such expectations still more directly: it begins with the setting up of a wedding and suggests the old conjunction of cup and cakes, but here there is no procession to or from church. A generation later again, a speech in another play, Beaumont and Fletcher's *The Scornful Lady*, fills out the scene but suggests that the eating and drinking was then occurring before the marriage had been formally made:

Lady   Beleeve me; if my wedding smock were on,
   Were the gloves bought and given, the licence come,
   Were the Rosemary branches dipt, and all
   The Hipochrists and cakes eate and drunke off,
   Were these two armes incompest with the hands
   Of Bachelors, to leade me to the Church;
   Were my feete in the dore, were *I John*, said
   If *John* should boast a favour done by me,
   I would not wed that yeare. . . .

The Kenilworth cakes were obviously something special. Their size, and the source of so much wheat for flour, were matters to be remarked on. They may well have been baked in the castle oven, though for less exceptional occasions it is likely that cakes, if any were produced at all, would have been of the simple, girdle-baked kind exemplified by the 'dumb cake' above. Aubrey's account of bride cakes in the first half of the

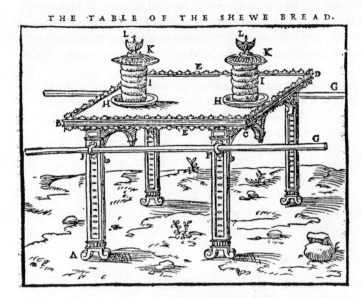

THE TABLE OF THE SHEWE BREAD.

Figure 1 Shewbread from the Geneva Bible (1560)

seventeenth century suggests the latter: 'When I was a little boy (before the Civill Warres) I have seen (according to the custome then) the Bride and Bride-groome kisse over the Bride-cakes at the Table: it was about the later end of dinner: and yᵉ cakes were layd one upon another, like the picture of the Sew-bread in yᵉ old Bibles' (Aubrey 1881: 22).[7] (See Figure 1.) Such cakes might, according to John Selden (1726: col. 668), seventeenth-century jurist and one of Aubrey's sources, either be made by the couple themselves or be provided by neighbours and friends.[8]

From Aubrey's report it can safely be inferred that what had been happening when he was a boy was not what he was familiar with as an adult. As one concerned with strange survivals, he does not tell us what that was but there is clear evidence elsewhere for some aspects of it. The key is probably in the frequent identification of cakes as 'great', as at Newbury and Kenilworth. The lexicographers record the term 'great cake' from the sixteenth century (Baret 1580; Withals 1608; probably Huloet 1552), and a hint as to what such cakes looked like is provided by Baret. He lists under 'cake': 'a great cake such as be at churchings and weddings'; and he gives the Latin for this as: '*Sumunalia*': '*Liba farinacea in modum rotae facta*'. This is actually a slightly misspelled version of a Roman definition. It is not, therefore, necessarily describing the cakes of the sixteenth century as 'made in the form of a wheel'. It may well be doing so however, for there is no reason otherwise why *Summanalia*, a cake offered to the Roman god Summanus and with no connection with 'churchings and weddings', should be identified with the 'great cakes' in question.[9]

How would such great cakes have been made? It is clear that there was not then, and has never been since, any fixed and essential recipe. A bride cake was a cake used for a wedding rather than a particular kind of cake. But there were already available suitable published recipes which begin a series displaying marked continuities which can be examined today. Gervase Markham, for instance, in *The English House-wife*, originally published in 1615 and going through a series of subsequent editions, offers a recipe for spice cakes. Whether the 'spisecakes' at Kenilworth forty years before would have been so rich is doubtful; it is not for any country bride-ale that he was catering. In a section of his work headed 'Skill in banqueting stuffe', distinguished from ordinary 'Skill in cookery', he writes:

> To make excellent spice Cakes, take half a pecke of very fine Wheat-flower [= c. 7lbs], take almost a pound of sweet butter, and some good milke and creame mixt together, set it on the fire, and put in your butter, and a good deale of sugar, and let it melt together: then strain Saffron into your milke a good quantity: then take seven or eight spoonefulls of good Ale-barme, and eight egges with two yelkes and mix them together, then put your milk to it when it is somewhat cold, and into your flower put salt, Aniseedes bruised, Cloves and Mace, and a good deale of Cinnamon: then work all together goode and stiffe, then you need not work in any flower after: then put in a little Rosewater cold, then rub it well in the thing you knead it in, and worke it thoroughly: if it be not sweete enough, scrape in a little more sugar, and pull it all in peeces, and hurle in a good quantity of Currants, and so worke all together againe, and bake your cake as you see cause in a gentle warm oven.
>
> (Markham 1615: 129)

Though the result would to modern eyes be more like an enriched bread than a cake, we already have here the term applied to a sweet, baked and raised food, the ancestor of the plum cake.

ALTERNATIVES AND THEIR PERSISTENCE

The cake developed therefore not as an integral part of any meal but as a festive or celebratory elaboration of bread. It was much later and in a very different world that it was worked into a pattern with other foods as part of the distinctively British afternoon tea or teatime. There have been other food items which have been associated with weddings but these have not owed their origins to celebration in any such direct manner. They have either been, like the cake subsequently, prepared in elaborated versions specifically for wedding feasts or they have been more or less ordinary foods given a special use in the wedding context.

The earliest recipe recorded from Britain for a dish specifically for a wedding is in fact a pie. The source is Robert May, who was trained as a cook in England and in France in the early seventeenth century and who served in such grand kitchens as the Grocers' Hall and the Star Chamber, as well as in various noble houses. After the Restoration of 1660 he set out to write a cookery book, *The Accomplish't Cook, or the Art and Mystery of Cookery*, which would revive the entertaining cookery of the banquets and the grand establishments he had known in the years before the Civil War. His book provides classics of fanciful elaboration and surprise, and these include 'an extraordinary Pie, or a Bride Pye'. The idea here was to make pies within pies. He shows a design in the shape of a Tudor rose, made up of four eight-petalled shapes, one within another. His instructions are to a degree ambiguous but his list of ingredients is sufficiently startling in itself. They include cock-stones[10] and combs, or lamb-stones and sweet breads of veal, two or three ox pellets blanched and sliced, a pint of oysters, a little quantity of broom-buds pickled, and pickled barberries (the fruit of the berberis). These, with other ingredients, were to be baked in a 'lear' of butter, egg yolks, wine and lemon juice.

> You may bake the middle [pie] full of flour, it being baked and cold, take out the flour in the bottom, and put in live birds or a snake, which seem strange to the beholders, which cut up the Pie at the Table. This is only for a wedding to pass away time.[11]
>
> (May 1665: no pagination)

This was both grand and eccentric. Whether it was ever tried is unknown. What is certain is that a tradition of bride's pies did exist and persisted long enough at least in the peripheries to be recorded in the rush of writing on old customs which began in the early nineteenth century. A minister from Jedburgh in the Borders between Scotland and England, writing in 1813–14, reported that at penny weddings – that is to say ones at which the guests paid for the entertainment and which were still, despite official hostility, being held in his time – the bride's pie was the principal dish in a plentiful dinner (Somerville 1861: 347). He does not describe the dish further; it may have been nothing more special than a mutton pie, as reported later but in the somewhat similar context of bidding weddings from the Gower peninsula in Wales (Tibbott 1986: 48–9). But a striking account from the Skipton area of North Yorkshire suggests that perhaps it was not:

> *Bride's-pie* The bride's pie was so essential a dish on the dining table, after the celebration of a marriage, that there was no prospect of happiness without it. This was always made round, with a very strong crust, ornamented with various devices. In the middle of it, the grand essential was a fat laying hen, full of eggs, probably intended as an emblem of fecundity. It was also garnished with minced and sweet meats. It would have been deemed an act of neglect or rudeness if any of the party omitted to partake of it. It was the etiquette for the bridegroom always to wait on this occasion on his bride.
>
> (Carr 1828: 51)

In Scotland it was a straightforward mince pie in the plum tradition noted above which reached the recipe books at much the same period. Since Christmas was little celebrated there, it was perhaps more available as a bride's pie than in England. Caird (1809: 393–4), who had a confectionery and grocery shop in Edinburgh, offers a 'Rich Calf's Feet Pye' and comments that 'when this is made in a tin shape, a glass ring put into the middle, covered, finely ornamented and baked, and turned out upon a dish, it is named the bride's pye, from an old adage that the lady who gets the ring will be the first bride of the party'. This does not necessarily imply that it was a wedding dish, but subsequent developments make it appear likely that it was: see also p. 75 below. Mrs Frazer, the author of the very successful *The Practice of Cookery, Pastry, and Confectionary* [sic], added the recipe to her seventh edition in 1820. Since her first in 1791, she had been describing herself as a teacher of the arts of cookery, etc. in Edinburgh; in her nineteenth century editions, she added 'Confectioner'. She entitles the recipe simply 'A Bride's Pie':

> Boil two calf's feet, take the meat from the bones, and chop it very small; take a pound of beef suet and a pound of apples shred small; clean and pick a pound of currants; stone and chop a quarter of a pound of raisins, a quarter of an ounce of cinnamon, the same of mace and nutmeg, two ounces of candied citron, the same of lemon-peel cut thin, a glass of brandy and champaigne: cover a round, loose-bottomed pan with puff paste and put the meat into it; roll out the lid, and ornament it with paste leaves, flowers, figures, and a ring.

Mrs C.J. Johnstone, a learned Scottish lady who wrote her cookery under the pseudonym, taken from Scott, of Mistress Meg Dods, echoed her predecessors when she began her *Cook and Housewife's Manual* in 1826. This was a publication which ran through fourteen editions or more. By the 1870s it still included the Bride's Pie but the instructions for it had come to notice the presence of the wedding cake, often commercially produced, as a rival for it (Dods 1826: 1870 edn 428, 504). Subsequently, ousted by flooding anglicisation and the changes to be discussed below, the pie disappeared altogether. The ring, however, is still to be found in Scotland in Hallowe'en cakes, an invention of the confectionery trade of much later date.

If pies are the main item of distinctive wedding food to be found in the literature, an altogether different and contrasting idea may finally be cited. It was provided by the French nouvelle cuisine of the mid-eighteenth century. This soon had its British proponents, one of the most striking being George Dalrymple with his *Practice of Modern Cookery* (Edinburgh 1781). In his Preface he wrote:

> Cookery, like most other arts, has its theory, which is of essential use to a workman who knows how to work by rules laid down to him. There is a harmony of composition (if I may be allowed the expression) in cookery throughout, that the intelligent cook immediately perceives.... There are several excellent Treatises published, wherein you see the Ancient Cookery in a very perfect degree: but I trust that this work will show the Modern Manner, with its improvements, in no despicable light.

With recipe titles in French first and then English, he sought out the new and original and omitted the standard recipes of 'the Ancient Cookery'. For weddings he offers an alternative which highlights the totally different tradition across the Channel:

Crême à la Mariée – Bride-cream
Beat up the yolks of six eggs and two of the whites, with a little flour, some rasped lemon-peel, a few orange-flowers minced very fine, a little chocolate and macaroni-biscuit as the last, a pint of cream, and sugar to taste; boil it about a quarter of an hour, stirring continually; then pour it on a table-dish, and colour the top with a salamander [= a device using a heated iron plate].

(Dalrymple 1781: 374)

Whether or not the sophisticated of the day enjoyed bride-cream at their wedding meals, which is unknown, it lacked both traditional resonance and the potential for commercial exploitation. Its failure to reappear in the literature as it built up voluminously during the following century can scarcely surprise.

Away from the world of crêmes and even of confectioner's shops and bride's pies, older and plainer associations between weddings and baking persisted. The 'bridal bread' was still being baked and would continue to be – somewhere – for another century or even two. It would be used for the cake-breaking that was a favourite and long-lasting event in the rites of marrying. It is discussed in Chapter 8.

Part II

The making of the British wedding cake

5 Great cakes, plum(b) cakes and bride cakes

GREAT CAKES FOR WEDDINGS

The bread enriched in the bakeries of the mighty and becoming cake in the modern sense was undoubtedly always made in large units. Recipes when they appear are based on either a peck or a half peck of flour, the peck being a somewhat variable measure but equivalent to twelve to fourteen pounds. Enrichment may indeed have been called for primarily by demand for a great cake sufficiently special to grace the events of the emergent upper classes of the period. It seems at least clear that the use of great cakes moved upwards in society as they were elaborated.

The first recipe linked explicitly to a wedding was published in 1655. It is a development of Markham's cake of forty years before, doubled in size and made more special by being enclosed like a modern Scots black bun in a pastry case. It was made for the wedding of the daughter of one of the greatest families in the land, the Manners of Belvoir, and, since the bridegroom was born only in 1635, the wedding must have taken place not long before the recipe's publication.

> *The Countess of Rutlands Receipt for making the rare Banbury Cake, which was so much praised at her Daughters (the Right Honourable the Lady Chaworths) Wedding.*
>
> Imprimis.
>
> Take a peck of fine flower, and half an ounce of large Mace, half an ounce of Nutmegs, and half an ounce of Cinnamon, your Cinnamon and Nutmegs must be sifted through a Searce [= sieve], two pounds of Butter, half a score of Egges, put out four of the whites of them, something above a pint of good Ale-yeast, beat your Eggs very well and strain them with your Yeast, and a little warm water into your Flower, and stir them together, then put your Butter cold in little Lumps: The water you knead withall must be scalding hot, if you will make it good Paste, the which having done, lay the Paste to rise in a

warm Cloth, a quarter of an hour or there upon; then put in ten
pounds of Currans, and a little Musk and Ambergreece dissolved in
Rosewater, your Currans must be made very dry, or else they will
make your Cake heavy, strew as much Sugar finely beaten amongst
the Currans as you shall think the water hath taken away the
sweetness from them; break your Paste into little pieces, in a Kimnel
[= kitchen tub] or such like thing and lay a layer of Paste broken into
little pieces, and a layer of Currans, untill your Currans are all put in,
mingle the Currans and the Paste very well, but take heed of breaking
the Currans, you must take out a piece of Paste after it hath risen in
a warm Cloth before you put in the Currans to cover the top, and the
bottom, you must roul the Cover something thin, and the bottom
likewise, and wet it with Rose-water, and close them at the bottom of
the side, or the middle which you like best, prick the top and the sides
with a small long pin; when your Cake is ready to go into the Oven,
cut it in the midst of the sight [? = side] round about with a Knife an
inch deep, if your Cake is to be of a peck of meal, it must stand two
hours in the Oven, your Oven must be as hot as for Manchet [= the
best kind of loaves].

(Price 1655: 109–10)

FROM GREAT CAKES TO PLUM(B) CAKES

By the 1660s, cakes had certainly become popular in London society. In
1664 Pepys records a great cake sent to him by a timber merchant
tendering for the supply of elm to the Navy, and in 1667 another from a
rope-maker. He often notes the cakes he enjoyed on excursions, usually
with his wife but once even when he took a prostitute out. On several
occasions he took his friends to the Kake-house in Southampton
market-place.[1] This was a drive-in establishment; they 'there sat in the
coach with great pleasure and eat some fine cakes'. His household
always had a Twelfth cake, and it looks as if this was becoming a much
richer confection in the period: in January 1661 his servants could buy
'an excellent cake' for 12d., whereas in 1668, even made by their
cookmaid at home, it 'cost me near 20s.', almost 12d. a slice. He also
records bride cake, cake at a christening and cake for a house-warming.

In Mrs Price's book, there are five other recipes for other elaborate
but uncased cakes, another Banbury cake, 'a very good great Oxfordshire
cake', 'a singular Receipt for making a Cake', 'Mrs Shellys Cake', and
'Mrs Dukes Cake'. All have a high proportion of flour to fat and sugar
and use ale-yeast as a raising agent. All contain a similar range of
ingredients, with spices and dried fruit much in evidence. Herrick's

poem, 'The Bride-cake', which dates from the same period, shows that in some circles at least almonds as well as spice were already clearly associated with cakes for weddings, though they were absent from the Countess of Rutland's. In the same book Mrs Shelly's and Mrs Duke's cakes do include them, and they sometimes appear also in recipes in other books of the period (Wolley 1664: 5; Digbie 1669: 264).

In the eighteenth century, mixtures of the same kind acquired the generic title 'plum(b) cake'. Though it had been used earlier for particular recipes, a general term was needed only as other kinds of cake began to appear. Hannah Wolley in a book of *Rare Receipts* (1664: 89–90) had offered one 'To make Cakes without Plumbs'. In 1760 Hannah Glasse, in *The Compleat Confectioner*, was offering similar recipes for 'A rich great cake' – still echoing in its name the old tradition – but also for 'A plumb cake' and 'An ordinary plumb cake' (see also Nott 1733). The plum cake had become a standard item; the age when it had belonged in the realm of 'banquetting stuff' and 'rare receipts' was well past.

A major change in its nature was also under way. A first hint had been registered by the same Hannah Wolley almost a hundred years before when she offered a recipe for 'A cake with Almonds' (1664: 5). This had still been a yeast cake but it was on a modest scale and of a much less bready mixture: 1lb of butter and 12oz of sugar to 1½ lbs of flour. In the early part of the eighteenth century John Nott published a transitional recipe looking back to the past in its style and proportions but abandoning yeast in favour of a pint of new ale (Nott 1733). It was Hannah Glasse who then first offered a recipe of clearly modern style in the first edition of her innovative *The Art of Cookery Made Plain and Easy*, published by subscription in 1747. Though she includes some yeast cakes, pride of place is given to 'a rich cake' so large that it would, she comments, bake best in two hoops (Glasse 1747: 138–9). This would deserve quoting were it not so manifestly a simpler version of Elizabeth Raffald's explicitly named bride cake which is presented in detail in the following section. Suffice it to say here that, though there was great continuity of ingredients, the proportion of flour in her mixture was sharply reduced and the yeast as a raising agent omitted.

The old style of bready plum cake was on its way out, to be replaced by the kind of cake which has continued to be baked with little more than minor variations in proportions and ingredients up to the present. Flour, currants and spice have been mixed with butter, sugar and eggs. The proportion of egg white was normally reduced until the nineteenth century, as it was in Mrs Glasse's recipe. As regards spice, the exact set used has varied, with nutmeg the most constant. Mace and cinnamon invariably appear in the earlier recipes, but the latter has been much more rarely used since the eighteenth century. Until the middle of that century, the quantities of spices were large by modern standards, though the effect may not have been quite so fierce as would now be imagined; Wilson (1973: 286) has suggested that modern spices are likely to be of greater purity and fresher, therefore requiring smaller quantities for the same flavouring effect. Almonds have already been referred to; they have been prominent since the eighteenth century, either in sliced or ground form. Candied orange and lemon, and citron, made their appearance in the same century and became regular ingredients in the nineteenth, as did brandy. In the eighteenth century, wine of one kind or another might be alternative or additional, and in the nineteenth, Jamaica rum appeared. As well as the constant currants, raisins have appeared at times and sultanas from the early twentieth century, with glacé cherries a recent innovation, though they did have a dried forerunner in Francatelli's 'Plum Cake, or Wedding Cake' of 1862, which was also taken to America (Francatelli 1862: 98; Anon 1866: 205).

THE BRIDE CAKE

It was not as a rule until the nineteenth century that recipes were labelled 'bride cake' or its variants, though plum cakes certainly continued to be used for that purpose. Elizabeth Raffald, whose *The Experienced English Housekeeper*, 'with near 800 original receipts', was first published in 1769, had however, for the first time, offered something distinctive to which the name could be attached. Her cake was copied, with acknowledgement, by Borella, 'an ingenious foreigner' and 'head confectioner to the Spanish ambassador in England', when he published a book of his own, *The Court and Country Confectioner*, the following year. For a second edition two years later, however, he varied the recipe and suppressed the attribution, perhaps in response to protest from Mrs Raffald herself.

Hers is the most important single name in the history of the wedding cake – for reasons which will appear more clearly in the following chapter – and a notable one in the history of English cooking more generally. After service as a housekeeper in various grand families, she set up a confectionery shop in Market Place, Manchester, and wrote and published her book (see also Harland 1867; Raffald 1772). It included recipes for the confectionery she herself sold. After its second edition was exhausted, the rights were bought by a London publisher for the enormous sum of £1400. From 1769 to 1825, it went through some thirty-six editions, many of them pirated.

Her original recipe and some of the discussion accompanying it deserve to be quoted in full:

Chap. XI. Observations upon *Cakes*

As to Plumb-cake, Seed-cake, or Rice-cake, it is best to bake them in Wood Garths [= hoops], for if you bake them in either Pot or Tin, they burn the Out-side of the Cakes, and confine them so that the heat cannot penetrate into the Middle of your Cake, and prevents it from rising; bake all Kinds of Cake in a good Oven, according to the Size of your Cake, . . .

To make a *Bride Cake*.

Take four Pounds of fine Flour well dried, four Pounds of fresh Butter, two Pounds of loaf Sugar, pound and sift fine a quarter of an Ounce of Mace, the same of Nutmegs, to every Pound of Flour put eight Eggs, wash four Pounds of Currants, pick them well and dry them before the Fire, blanch a Pound of sweet Almonds (and cut them length-ways very thin), a Pound of Citron, one Pound of candied Orange, the same of candied Lemon, half a Pint of Brandy; first work the Butter with your Hand to a Cream, then beat in your Sugar a quarter of an Hour, beat the Whites of your Eggs to a very strong Froth, mix them with your Sugar and Butter, beat your Yolks half an Hour at least, and mix them with your Cake, then put in your Flour, Mace and Nutmeg, keep beating it well 'till your Oven is ready, put in your Brandy, and beat your Currants and Almonds lightly in, tie three Sheets of Paper round the Bottom of your Hoop to keep it from running out, rub it well with Butter, put in your Cake, and lay your Sweet-meats in three Lays, with Cake betwixt every Lay, after it is risen and coloured, cover it with paper before your Oven is stopped up; it will take three hours baking.

(Raffald 1769: 242–3)

This recipe, by modern standards somewhat low on fruit, almonds and sugar, high on butter and flour and with the peel put in distinctively in layers, was not, after Borella's abortive attempt, taken up directly by anyone else until well after Mrs Raffald's death in 1781. Henderson, in his *Housekeeper's Instructor* originally published in parts about 1793, then offered it almost word for word except that he, unlike Mrs Raffald, could with advances in baking technology recommend baking 'in a moderate oven'. Caird (1809: 137), a Scottish confectioner writing with the trade primarily in mind, offered a practically identical recipe, and Dolby, a professional restaurant cook in London, published the recipe verbatim and again without acknowledgement in his alphabetical

Cook's Dictionary and Housekeeper's Directory as late as 1830. It crossed
the Atlantic too, to reappear more than fifty years later again in an
American Home Confectionery Book, 'as prepared in both Americas and
the Indies' (F. 1888: 38).

In Britain, however, though the plum cake was unstoppable, a
somewhat puritan reaction had set in by the mid-century. Eliza Acton
avoided offering any such recipe, indeed minimised the cake section in
her *Modern Cookery for Private Families* (first published 1845). She
asserted that 'more illness is caused by habitual indulgence in the richer
and heavier kinds of cakes than would easily be credited by persons who
have given no attention to the subject. Amongst those which have the
worst effects are almond, and plum *pound* cakes, as they are called . . . '
(Acton 1873: 540–1). These were cakes for which the recipes showed an
almost ritual fascination with equal quantities of all the main
ingredients; for Elizabeth Raffald it was 4lbs and others have at times
taken the principle even further than she (see e.g. Hueg 1901: 27). Such
a procedure results in a rich cake. Mrs Beeton, when she began
publishing in 1861, registered the objection at least to the extent of
avoiding any single number and sharply increasing the proportion of
flour in the recipe she offered.

The move did not last. In the later years of the century, the proportion
of flour in such cakes retreated well below the levels of the eighteenth
century pioneers and the proportion of dried fruit, peel and almonds
rose to well over half. The wedding cake became the flagship of the
confectionery trade, with firms competing amongst themselves at trade
exhibitions and using their masterpieces as eye-catchers in window
displays and in their advertising (cf. Cox 1903: 23). A commercial recipe
published by one of the leading propagators of new products and new
styles, for the profitable advancement of the trade, catches the tone and
scale of its leaders towards the end of the century. It contains,
proportionately, twice the currants and almonds and half the butter and
flour that Mrs Raffald used. Mace as a spice had gone and citron was no
longer a featured ingredient. Otherwise, despite the larger scale of
production, it is still the clear descendant of the cake being sold in
Manchester in the eighteenth century.

Bride or Wedding Cake

20lb. best butter	90lb. currants
25lb. cane sugar	300 eggs
24lb. flour	1 bottle brandy
20lb. whole almonds	1 bottle Jamaica rum
40lb. mixed peel	4 oz. grated nutmeg

All ingredients must be of the finest quality procurable. Don't you forget it.

(Vine n.d.: 216)

This remains an essentially simple if lavish cake. As the final comment suggests, the temptation to use cheaper ingredients was always there and was undoubtedly important too. It offered the means whereby the wedding cake, in smaller and cheaper versions, was able to percolate widely through society even by the end of the nineteenth century. Cox (1903: 18–22) notes the variation in the quality of cakes being offered around the country. They were selling for between 7s. 6d. for a seven-inch cake – half the five-pound weight of this would be icing and decoration – to a guinea for a 10½-inch, 7lb cake. In the previous decade there had been cakes at a shilling a pound as well as the 1s. 6d. represented here (Gommez 1896: 21). There were also grand multi-tiered versions at far higher prices still, though they were not the kind of thing that most baker-confectioners were ever likely to have the chance to sell. As a contemporary French observer put it: 'Il est ainsi mis à la portée de toutes les bourses, depuis celle du plus humble citoyen justqu' à celle du lord richissme' (Suzanne 1894: 232–4).

Apart from offering relatively small cakes and reducing the quantities of high-cost ingredients, as the twentieth century went on, substitution focussed particularly on the fats and the almonds. Margarines might be substituted for the butter, or at least only as much butter would be used as was felt necessary to retain a distinctive contribution to flavour. Almonds might be substituted in whole or in part by essences. The shortages of the Second World War and the years immediately following stretched substitution to breaking point.

The twentieth century also saw a divergence between specifications for the commercial cake and for the home baker, which went beyond this simple question of quality. The commercial remained dominant; though greater numbers of home-bakers could aspire to the baking of large cakes, there were never many with the confidence and the skill to take on the full three tiers with the requisite royal-iced decoration. Nevertheless most general cookery books as well as more specialised books of cakes found it necessary to tell the amateur how a wedding cake was to be done. The old standards and the relatively simple ingredient lists were retained or reinstated in this mass of publication for home-bakers, but each needed something different to offer. There were cakes with marzipan in the mixture, with bitter almonds, with no spice, with French plums, with no peel, with orange juice, with no alcohol, with the zest of oranges or lemons, with caramel for colouring (Jack 1907;

Werlim 1915; Little 1929; Leyel 1936).[2] A proportion of self-raising flour might be used to lighten the cake. And for both commercial and amateur cakes in the twentieth century, to the currants and raisins came normally to be added sultanas and then glacé cherries.

Commercial production from the 1930s onwards, while responding to some of these trends too, was beginning to differentiate not merely with a usually cheaper product but with a technologically more complex one (Bennion & Stewart 1945). A high-quality commercial recipe of the 1980s (Littlewood 1989 (Part 2): 27) may be compared with Vine's above:

225g. cake margarine	270g. currants
225g. butter	670g. sultanas
450g. Barbados sugar	225g. seedless raisins
110g. wholemeal flour	530g. eggs
110g. plain flour	some rum
55g. ground almonds	10g. vanilla essence
15g. marzipan	3.5g. lemon oil
110g. chopped citron peel	28g. caramel colour
110g. chopped orange peel	zest + juice of small orange
3.5g. mixed spice	

Apart from the shift to metric measures somewhat disguising the relatively small scale of this second recipe, its greater complexity is clear. In its variety of fats, flours and dried fruits, the small proportion of the costly almonds, the presence of colouring and the multiplicity of flavouring substances it stands, despite its exalted nature, for the food of a more technology-dependent age.

In the old age of the twentieth century, the rich-fruit style retained its dominance: a small survey in 1990 suggested that well over 80 per cent of cakes were still entirely traditional in this respect. But other mixtures were becoming possible, sponges commonest but other kinds of fruit cake, madeira and even carrot cake were occasionally being ordered. The least unusual possibility (5 per cent) was a sponge top tier to an otherwise rich-fruit cake.

CAKES FOR WEDDINGS AND OTHER FESTIVITIES

There has never been any absolute separation between mixtures for wedding and other cakes. Up to the first half of the nineteenth century it was Twelfth cakes which were chiefly special enough to share the same rich mixture, perhaps with some marginal differentiation. Kitchiner claimed that bride cakes were generally distinguished by using raisins as well as currants (1823: 433–4), though somewhat earlier the Twelfth cake might still have been a yeast mixture and that, as has been seen, often had both kinds of dried fruit in it from the beginning (Caird 1809: 149). When Mrs Beeton started publication in 1861 she felt that the same cake would be appropriate for christenings as for weddings (Beeton 1861: 854). In the twentieth century, silver and golden weddings were increasingly likely to be celebrated with a similar cake. The Christmas cake, when it replaced the Twelfth cake in the mid-nineteenth century, remained much the same but often with less of the fruits and nuts and spices and alcohols which were so prominent in wedding-cake mixtures. As a cake needed regularly by every family, and increasingly attainable, it was also far more likely to be baked at home. Birthday cakes might still in the nineteenth century be of the same kind, but as their use spread, their composition became typically simpler. For birthdays indeed, any mixture might be chosen, according to the preference of the child or other person celebrating, or of the cook, or whatever the confectioner had used for a decorated shop cake.

In the 1980s the birthday trade expanded with a profusion of 'novelty' cakes in the form of objects and people, in themselves amusing or with some reference to the interests of the birthday person. Similar cakes but on a grander scale were increasingly common, in advertising and to be ceremonially cut for the inauguration of buildings and public events, as well as for such personal events as engagement, home-coming or retirement. Cakes for events were on an upward curve throughout the century but, with the exception of the wedding cake, the focus in Britain had left the mixture and shifted entirely to the outward decorated form.

It has been the requirement for something special for weddings, the best, that has most consistently determined the cake used. When the plum cake was the only cake available, whatever festivity called for a cake it was bound to be a plum cake. As types of cake proliferated, at first only by variation on the plum-cake theme but then by the importation of the very different sponge tradition from the continent, choice gained scope. Tradition, the fact that the plum cake was already associated with festivity, might not have been sufficient to retain its association, but this was reinforced by the criterion of expense: the old cake was the best not just because it was old but because it was composed of the most costly ingredients. As such however, other cake uses tended to pull away from it, leaving it and its association with weddings increasingly distinctive. It might indeed, as has been seen, be further elaborated: not one candied peel would be needed but three, not one dried fruit but three, not one flavour to be added but three, and sometimes not one alcohol where two would do. Sometimes special

methods for applying them were developed too. The cake retained for
weddings was therefore the spiced and alcoholised, fruit and almond
cake in substantially the form it reached in the eighteenth century. It was
subsequently kept at the head of the field with appropriate additions and
elaborations.

Such a cake, in contrast to cakes in the continental tradition, could
be kept. There is no reason to think that it was constructed in order to
be kept, merely that the object as it evolved had this potential. It is not
the keeping quality of the dry biscuit however; the moisture in a cake
ensures that it will not be inert but will change over time. Where changes
reduce the initially attractive qualities of a cake it is said to be going
stale, a state short of becoming inedible or going bad. A rich fruit cake
changes, however, as the moisture diffuses more evenly through the
mixture. This may be regarded not as the loss of its fresh qualities but as
an improvement. Both texture and flavour and ease of cutting may
improve, and the process may be dignified as 'maturing'. As with wines
and cheeses, the concept and the practice have the effect of elevating
whatever they are applied to into a special realm of gustatory excellence.
As applied to the wedding cake it has a special extra relevance. It makes
of the cake in this tradition not a thing of the moment, to be, like the
continental cake, quickly prepared and quickly consumed, but
something enduring. Most striking has been the idea often found in the
twentieth century that the top tier should be kept for the (first)
christening. The beginning of this idea is so far undocumented, but
whether or not it was the trade that originated it, they have often given
it support by offering to re-ice cakes kept for such a purpose.

The intentional maturing of cakes was taken up, and perhaps actually
invented, by the confectionery trade. Messrs W. Hill of London,
Purveyors to Her Majesty, suggested their own creativity in the matter
when they featured it in the introduction to their special catalogue of
1879:[3]

> For nearly a century past, the firm have been celebrated for the
> excellence of Wedding Cakes, of which they are, perhaps, the largest
> manufacturers. They, therefore, venture to remind the public of a fact
> but little known, viz., that rich Cakes require to be kept for six
> months, in order to be thoroughly matured and in the best possible
> state. It is needless to say that there are few confectioners who have
> either time, plant, capital, or space necessary to ensure this most
> essential condition.
>
> Messrs. Hill never send out their Cakes until they have matured the
> full time, and hence attained the highest state of perfection. Their

cakes, 'richly almond-iced and ornamented, decorated with flowers, sprays, wreaths, &c.' cost from a guinea to £25.

Though there was an element of special pleading here, the idea of maturing was widely accepted, if not for the generous period it suited Messrs Hill to claim. Even by the 1980s it was unusual to find a firm boldly denying, as did the leading supplier in the West of Scotland at that time, that there was any merit in keeping cakes at all.

6 Confectionery and icing

SUGARPASTE AND THE BEGINNINGS OF CONFECTIONERY

Master Alexis of Piedmont, whose 'Secretes' were translated into English, stylishly printed and published in 1558, offers instruction

> To make a paste of sugre, wherof a man maye make all maner of fruites, and other fyne thynges, with theyr forme, as platters, dishes, glasses, cuppes, and such like thinges, wherwith you may furnish a table: and when you have doen, eate them up. A pleasant thing for them that sit at the table.
>
> Take gomme dragant [= gum tragacanth, or 'gum dragon' as it was sometimes called], as much as you will, and stiepe it in Rose water, untill it be molified. And for foure onces of Sugre, take of it the bignes of a Beane, the iuyce of Lemons a walnut shell full, and a litle of the white of an egge: but you must first take the gomme, and beate it so much with a pestel in a morter of white marble, or of brasse untill it become like water, then put to it the iuyce with the white of the egge, incorporating wel altogether. This dooen, take iiii. onces of fine white sugre, well beaten to poulder, and cast it into the morter by litle and litle, untill all bee turned into the forme of paste. Then take it oute of the saied morter, and bray it upon the poulder of sugre, as it were meale or flowre, untill all bee like soft paste, to the ende you may turne it and facion it which way you wil. Whan you have brought your paste to this forme, spreade it abroade with Sinamon, upon greate or small leaves, as you shall thinke it good: and so shall you forme and make what things you wil, as is aforesated. [. . .] this paste is verie delicate and savourous.
>
> (Alexis 1558: 64–5)

We are here probably fairly near to the beginning of sugarpaste in Britain. Alexis's book was widely translated from the original Italian and was repeatedly and extensively plagiarised. Sugar boiling to produce 'sugar plate' was older, and this substance was also, though less flexible than sugarpaste, used to make images. These might be gilded, silvered or coloured (Hieatt & Butler 1985: 152–3) and were doubtless the main form of sugar used in the subtleties discussed in Chapter 4. In Italy and elsewhere, however, the new material was taken up with enthusiasm, as a medium for artistic productions, sometimes of almost the highest quality. Between the late fifteenth and the first half of the eighteenth centuries, these reached new heights in 'trionfi di tavola' for grand events such as the weddings of the Medicis and papal banquets for visiting royalty. The trionfi for these were the work of well-known sculptors and often closely resembled the bronzes of the period, a high art in sugar (Masson 1966: 338–41; Watson 1978: 20–6).

MARCHPANES

In England, however, from the later sixteenth century it comes to be marchpanes rather than subtleties which feature in the record, perhaps partly because this record is increasingly filled out with more than descriptions of extraordinary and famous events, the peaks of royal and noble entertaining. Marchpanes were also ancient: Alexis mentions them but without the detail or the enthusiasm he lavishes on sugarpaste. Marchpane was a paste of almonds and sugar, and confections of it came to form a highlight of rich and elaborate eating, particularly in the increasingly prosperous century between the English Reformation and the Civil War. The *OED*'s first reference to a decorated marchpane dates, however, from 1494. Half a century later a hundred of them were bought in, at a cost of 6d., for a marriage feast held at Ingatstone Hall in Essex in June 1552. They were 'wrought with no small curiositie' (Emmison 1964: 52).

The Treasurie of hidden Secrets (Partridge 1596: no pagination) offers instructions for their preparation. Chapter 1 is 'To make marchpane': it is a compound of ½lb blanched almonds, ground, with ¼lb white sugar, and a little rose water and damaske water. Once this 'geare' had been prepared

> Then take wafer cakes of the broadest making, cut them square, paste them together with a little liquor, and when you have made them as broad as will serve your purpose, have ready made a hoop of a green hazell wand, of the thicknesse of halfe an inch, on the inner side smooth, without any knags: lay this hoop upon your Wafer cakes aforesaid, and then fill your hoop with the geare above named, the same driven smooth above with the backe of a silver spoone, as yee

doe a Tart, and cut away all the partes of the cakes, even close by the ouitside of the hoop, with a sharp knife, that it may be round.

The marchpane is then heated, not to bake it but to dry it thoroughly.

ye may while it is moyst stick it full of Comfrets of sundry collours, in a comely order, ye must moist it over with Rose water and sugre together: make it smooth, and so set it into the oven or other Instrument, the clearer it is like a Lantern horne so much the more commended. . . . The greatest secret that is in making this cleare, is with a little fine flower of Rice, Rosewater, and sugre beaten togither, and laid thin over the Marchpane ere it goe to drying. This will make it shine like yce, as Ladies report.

The decoration of marchpanes might be taken further. Like sugar plate before them (Hieatt & Butler 1985: 153), they might be gilded and perhaps silvered, though not apparently coloured. Partridge continues:

Chapter 2   *To gild a Marchpane, or any other kind of tart.*
Take and cut your leafe of gold, as it lyeth upon the book, into square peces like dice, and with a Conies tayls and moisted a litle, take the gold by the one corner, lay it on the place, being first made moist, and with another tayle of a Conie drie, presse the gold down close. And if you will have the form of an Hart, or the name of Jesus, or any other strange thing whatsoever, cut the same through a peece of paper, and lay the paper upon your Marchpan, or tart: then make the void place of the paper moist with Rosewater, lay on your golde, presse it downe, take off your paper and there remaineth behind in gold, the print cut in the said paper.

It is clear in this work that marchpane was both a substance and a particular confection made from it. As a substance it contrasted with sugarpaste, for his account of which our author makes free with Master Alexis's text already quoted. As a confection, it could take a wider range of forms than is suggested here. The paste could be stamped out or shaped at will, spices could be added to it and candied fruits incorporated into it. It could, as in the instructions above, be put on wafers, and it could be iced and decorated. Sir Hugh Platt's *Delightes for Ladies, to adorne their persons, tables, closets and distillatories* (1603: no pagination) offers more elaborate styles of decoration. One of his marchpanes is to be iced as soon as it comes out of the oven, and then put back in again to set the icing. That done, it is to be garnished 'with prettie conceiptes, as birds and beasts being cast out of standing moldes. Stick long confits [= crystallised or otherwise sugared fruits, etc.]

upright in it, cast bisket and carrowayes in it, and so serve it; guild it before you serve it.'

Marchpanes were, therefore, at this period a chief celebration food. Icing was developed first and foremost for them, and they might even be further decorated on the icing. Gervase Markham (1615: 136) comments that, in arranging a banquet, 'March-panes have the first place, the middle place, and the last place.' They had by this time become proverbial as the expression of all that was most delicious and exquisite.

They were never altogether forgotten (Caird 1809: 165) and they have some relevance to eventual wedding-cake developments, even if this was less than has sometimes been claimed (Wilson 1973: 270–1). Though they were further elaborated (e.g. Digbie 1669: 266–7), they did not hold their own well in competition with the host of sweet dishes which were developed and which joined the repertoire between the late seventeenth and the early nineteenth centuries. The term itself assumed a variety of forms reflecting successive reintroductions from the continent. Borella, writing his *The Court and County Confectioner* in 1770, offers only French-style almond-paste items and introduces an appropriately French term for them, *'massepins'* (see also Francatelli 1862: 114). Eventually, large-scale importing of 'marzipan' from Germany in the later nineteenth century is said to have resulted in a standardisation on that German form of the name. Applied to cakes, however, it was a rather different substance that first established itself as 'almond icing' or 'almond paste', and the two streams for long remained terminologically separate. The first testimony to this application comes from Mrs Raffald in 1769, but before considering that, the history of icing itself needs attention.

THE DEVELOPMENT OF ICING

Though cake icing had begun, perhaps only in the highest circles, in the seventeenth century, until the early nineteenth century if anything were to be iced it was most likely to be marchpanes in the early period, tarts rather later. Only a simple glazing was involved when the term 'ice' first began to be used. The earlier decorated marchpanes already referred to were, as has been seen, to be washed over with a rosewater syrup before being put into the oven 'for that will make the Ice'. The same could, however, also be done with a cake as soon as it came out of the oven. If you then put it in again to dry, 'when you draw it out it will shew like Ice' (Price 1655: 115).

The addition of white of egg was the beginning of new things and there was always more than one possibility. In another of her recipes,

Rebecca Price directs the cook to 'frost' the newly baked cake over with the white of an egg beaten together with rosewater 'and strew fine Sugar upon it, and then set it again into the Oven that it may Ice' (1655: 13). Yet another is to be iced with the same ingredients plus a little butter but put onto the unbaked cake. Sir Kenelm Digbie's collection published, posthumously, only fourteen years later represents a large and precocious step forward (Digbie 1669: 258–64). Rather than collecting up the recipes of named ladies, as Price tended to do, Digbie provides a rather systematic set of variations, proceeding from 'To make a Cake' through 'To make a Plumb-Cake' to 'To make an Excellent Cake'. For icing he includes, in addition to recipes of earlier style, three for which the later name of 'royal icing' would clearly be appropriate. His basic recipe and a variant deserve quotation:

> Then take a pound and a half of double refined Sugar purely beaten and searsed; put into the whites of five Eggs; two or 3 spoonfuls of rose-water; keep it beating all the time that the cake is baking which will be two hours; Then draw your Cake out of the oven, and pick the dry currants from the top of it, and so spread all that you have beaten over it, very smooth, and set it a little into the oven, that it may dry.

The hours of beating were to be a characteristic requirement for this extravagant form of icing. The proportion of egg white to sugar was more variable, one egg – doubtless variable in size but probably small by modern standards – for between two and eight ounces of sugar. With variable additions of other liquids too, it is difficult to know without detailed experiment, which has not been done, how different the results achieved would have been.

Digbie offers a further interesting variant. This adds spice, as do most of his recipes, and has other additional elements too.

> Then to Ice it, take a pound and half of double refined Sugar beaten and searsed; The whites of three Eggs new-laid, and a little Orange flower-water, with a little Musk and Ambergreece, beaten and searsed, and put to your sugar; Then strew your Sugar into the Eggs, and beat it in a stone Mortar with a Woodden Pestel, till it be a white as snow, which will be by the time the cake is baked; Then draw it to the oven mouth, and drop it on, in what form you will; let it stand a little again in the oven to harden.

This recognition of further decorative possibilities in the stiffened mixture seems to have been entirely exceptional, not even to be taken up by subsequent writers until it was exploited for piping in the nineteenth century.

Digbie, in the course of a life eventful even by the standards of his eventful times, lived and travelled extensively on the continent. It is possible therefore that his ideas about icing derived from experience abroad. Wheaton (1983: 177), writing on French cookery, says that a royal icing was being used in France by the mid-seventeenth century. In Britain however, it is clear that the icing of cakes took time to establish its popularity, even amongst the expanding cake-making and sugar-buying classes of the eighteenth century.

For those who did use it, the procedures and proportions given by Digbie were usually more or less maintained. The spicing of icings was, however, already on its way out in the eighteenth century. A simple version, merely a pound of sugar to the whites of seven eggs, was offered by the first Scottish cookery book (McLintock 1736). Mrs Glasse in London, in the first edition in 1747 of her famous book, was still trying to follow Digbie (see above) for her basic recipe;[1] by her third in 1755 it had been abandoned. Starch began occasionally to feature at the same period. It was often taken up subsequently and came to be added to commercial icing powder when this began to be manufactured in the mid-nineteenth century. Also in the nineteenth, lemon juice was substituted for the earlier flower-waters and the passion for whiteness projected some into including powder blue.

The concern with whiteness had been explicit, despite the somewhat different initial connotations of the term 'ice', since icings in the modern sense developed out of glazes. Icing was, until much more recent times, an item of lavish display in itself, its whiteness a direct indicator of the quality and expense of the sugar from which it was produced (Mintz 1985: 77–8, 87). As late as 1809, Caird begins a detailed practical account of 'Icing for all Manner of Cakes, Biscuits, etc.' with the assertion that 'In proportion to the quality of the sugar will be the whiteness of the icing, or glazing; therefore, it requires double, or triple refined sugar, to make a pure white icing'. By then, colouring was a possibility, as it had not been at the earlier period, and for that 'an inferior sugar' could be used. By then too, perhaps with a change in the ovens used, he was ready to assert: 'Cakes should never be put into an oven after being iced, the heat being far too great, which either occasions the icing to run off, or cracks and discolours it' (1809: 149–50).

Modification was made over time therefore, and there was some more radical experimentation continuing too. Hannah Glasse tried adding starch and some gum tragacanth as 'another way to Ice a great Cake' in the confused entry of her first edition. In her third, 'To Ice a Great Cake' she proposed something altogether different, twenty-four whites to one pound of sugar, put onto a cold cake: 'It does not do well hot.' This would then be placed in a cool oven and kept turning to avoid a change of colour. The effect would have been what in modern terms would have been a soft meringue rather than icing (Glasse 1755: 272).[2] She had her followers towards the end of the century (Henderson 1793: 229) and in the next Mrs Rundell (1824: 320), but she herself, by the time she wrote her specialised confectionery book (1760), had thought better of it. The author of a slightly later confectionery compendium does, however, offer something new again, what would now be recognised as a fondant icing. He had learnt his trade in a fashionable London confectioners and it seems likely that, despite proclaiming himself as offering 'a ready assistant to all genteel families', it was a commercial rather than a domestic procedure which he presents:

> Take six whites of eggs and whisk them very strong; then have a pint of syrup in a small stewpan, and let the syrup boil until it comes to blow through your skimmer; work it about the pan with a spoon, when it is all white and is a good deal thicker, mix the whites of eggs together, make it very thick, put it over your cakes and put them in your stove, let them dry, then put another coat over them. . . .
>
> (Nutt 1789: 100–1)

Even in the eighteenth century there had therefore been a good deal of experimentation. Fondant icing was available but mixtures normally termed 'royal icing' remained the standard in Britain. Though suitable for decorating, many thought it less than ideal on other grounds. Despite making his name by the use of such icing at the end of the next century, Herr Willy – as he seems always to have wanted to be known – a London cake decorator and writer and teacher of piping, did not lose his continental scorn for the substance. He did his best to deny it the title 'royal'; it was, he said, merely 'whites icing' (Willy 1891: 15). 'The only drawback in the use of Royal Icing for cakes, is that it sets very hard, and is not particularly nice to eat' (Lewis & Bromley 1903). Whether these are its only drawbacks might today be contested, but a solution to the former problem had already been sought in the addition of glycerine (Heritage 1894: 1015). As regards the latter, the versions of earlier centuries may sometimes have been preferable, but both the material and its use were set in Britain to last for another century yet.

DOUBLE ICING

It was Mrs Raffald in 1769 who published directions for covering a cake first with a layer of almond icing and then with white. In a sense, ever since the days of iced marchpanes there had been little to invent here and that little had largely been filled in with the development of royal icing. But it needs to be stressed that it was not marchpane or marzipan but a variant of icing which Mrs Raffald was proposing. The evidence suggests that it was her own idea, probably as a novelty for selling in her shop in Manchester. The combination, though it would later be applied to other kinds of cakes, certainly began with the bride cake and stands at the beginning of its differentiation from plum cakes generally.

Mrs Raffald's recipe for the cake itself was quoted in Chapter 4 above. On its covering she wrote:

> To make *Almond Iceing* for the *Bride Cake*
> Beat the whites of three Eggs to a strong Froth, beat a Pound of Jordan Almonds very fine with Rose Water, mix your Almonds with the Eggs lightly together, a Pound of common Loaf Sugar beat fine, and put in by Degrees, when your Cake is enough, take it out and lay your Iceing on, and put it in to Brown.

> To make *Sugar Iceing* for the *Bride Cake*
> Beat two pounds of double refined Sugar, with two ounces of fine Starch, sift it through a Gawze Sieve, then beat the Whites of five Eggs with a Knife upon a Pewter Dish half an Hour, beat in your Sugar a little at a Time, or it will make the Eggs fall, and will not be so good a colour, when you have put in all your Sugar, beat it half an Hour longer, then lay it on your Almond Iceing, and spread it even with a Knife; if it be put on as soon as the Cake comes out of the Oven, it will be hard by that Time the Cake is cold.

> (Raffald 1769: 243–4)

These two icings are similar in both being compounds of beaten egg white and sugar. They diverge with the addition of almond in the one case, in the other of starch. The way they are then to be treated makes a further contrast but this, it should be noticed, derives partly from established procedures. Like most icings before it, the first to be put on goes onto a hot cake. The iced cake is then put back into a still relatively hot oven, but with the difference here that it is explicitly to brown what would otherwise be no more than a pale yellowish substance. The white icing can then still be put onto a hot cake but it will not now be returned to the oven. Its whiteness will contrast with the browned layer below it.

Mrs Raffald's scheme continued to be published in successive editions and certainly found its way into many housekeepers' collections (White 1932: 330–2), but it was strikingly ignored by other authors for almost a century. Of those who followed her book most closely, Borella (1770/1772), whom we have already met, took up her almond icing but ignored the larger scheme of which it had been a part, as did Henderson (1793: 229) who gave it as an alternative to the egg-rich meringue style which he had taken from Mrs Glasse. It was not until the 1860s that writers acknowledged double icing. By then it had clearly become established, and Mrs Beeton noted what was presumably domestic practice. Of her 'Rich Bride or Christening Cake' she notes: 'These cakes are usually spread with a thick layer of almond icing, and over that another layer of sugar icing, and afterwards ornamented' (1861: 854). Her almond icing was of Mrs Raffald's kind and was carried by her famous publication in successive editions right through to the present. Rather different substances were however already being used to fulfil the double-icing prescription.

Francatelli, trained in France and employed in the household of Queen Victoria herself, proposes using a thick layer of an elaborate form of cooked marzipan.

> When the plum cake is cold, and cleared of the paper, and trimmed, place it on a baking sheet, and cover the top with a coating of orgeate paste, No. 226, one inch and a half in thickness, and dry this in the screen for an hour; then, cover the whole surface of the cake with a coating of royal icing, No. 202, about half an inch in thickness.

His No. 226 was to be prepared thus:

> Boil a pound of sugar to the crack, add fourteen ounces of almond pulp, stir all together with a wooden spoon over a slow fire until the paste ceases to adhere to the sides of the pan, and then work in half an ounce of prepared gum dragon with more icing sugar on the slab.
> (Francatelli 1862: 89)

The previous year Jeanes, the chief confectioner of Gunters of Berkeley Square in London, 'Confectioners to her Majesty', had published a still more elaborate recipe of the same kind, though he still called it 'almond icing for the wedding cake' (Jeanes 1861: 205).

MARZIPAN

From this time onwards the double icing for wedding cakes was to be taken for granted, but professional and commercial caterers were leading the way to a substitution of marzipans, which might also be called 'almond paste', for icing in the scheme. These were substances, more or less plastic according to the method of preparation, which could be rolled out and attached to the cake – with gum arabic, egg white or later sieved apricot jam or purée – rather than spread on as an icing. In the twentieth century it has often been thought important to achieve a strong colour and for this purpose yolks, in contrast to the whites used alone in the icing, and even yellow colouring were often prescribed (Littlewood 1989, Part 3: 23–5). A stronger flavour was often preferred too: artificial almond essence might therefore be added and the way was opened to cheap substitutes for the always costly almonds. A reduced proportion of almonds might be helped out with essence, or the almonds might even disappear altogether.

In the nineteenth century, however, there is one other possibility to which marzipan gave rise. It is thoroughly explained in an article excerpted in *The British Baker* (Vol. IX, 1892/3: 393):

> *Wedding-Cakes: New Style* – Who (asks 'Hill' in 'The Gentle- woman') was the inventor of the new wedding-cakes? Whoever he was he deserves immortalising, for his was a brilliant idea, one I should have been 'real proud of' myself had I thought of it. In the wedding-cake of more ancient type there was always a thick layer of white sugar which nobody cared about; a medium layer of almond paste, which everybody wished for, and did not always get; and an immense quantity of cake of which many only ate a few crumbs. The latest specimen has a thin layer of sugar, only just enough to look pretty, and underneath are alternate layers of cake and almond paste, one as thick as the other. The consequence is that no one is defrauded of their lawful share of almond paste, or 'love' as it is usually called, and for purposes of distribution it is far better, as the contents of the box does not crumble away nearly so much as it did when the principal portion was cake alone. If only someone would invent a box which could not be rifled, and was bound to reach its lawful destination, we should have nothing left to desire!

'New' this may have in a sense been, for the simnel cake as a marzipan Easter speciality was also a product of commercial initiative at the same period, but what is described here was just what Jeaffreson termed 'our grandest piece of confectionery' twenty years earlier. It was indeed 'the layers of almond paste which divide the plum-work' which he took to be the ancient and defining characteristic of such cakes. At a time when cakes had not yet risen in tiers, he saw the layers as properly to be regarded 'less as material for the enrichment of the composition than as memorials of the time when the wedding-cake consisted of several cakes, each of which had its coating of almond sweet-meat or sugar-ice' (1872: 209).[3]

DECORATION AND COLOUR

Icing is one thing, the addition of an almond layer another, and a third is colour and other kinds of decoration on the icing. Early on, when an iced plumb cake was already a costly and labour-intensive achievement, further decoration seems rarely, in contrast with the decoration of marchpanes, to have been considered. Hannah Wolley (1664: 90) had, it is true, suggested strewing her 'Cake without Plumbs' with comfits, but this was merely glazed, not iced. Suitable sugarpaste ornaments were even available (Eales 1718: 66). But the fifth edition of Mrs Frazer's *Practice of Cookery, Pastry and Confectionery*, published in 1806, is the earliest explicit account of cake ornamentation I have found. Having given instructions for icing the cake all over, she continues:

> If you choose to ornament the cake, put a Crown in the middle, and other small fancy figures on the top; waving small shells up and down the sides of it, and placing within the crown a bunch of artificial flowers of different colours; the crown, figures and shells are of sugarpaste, the flowers and leaves of different coloured paste, and the stalks of lemon peel.
>
> (Frazer 1806: 202)

Caird, again from the Edinburgh area and clearly reporting commercial practice, followed quick on Mrs Frazer's heels and with a more revealing discussion (1809: 150). After icing 'a high shaped cake, such as a gato, or obelisk', it is, he says,

> immediately ornamented with spangles, gold and silver leaf, drague, mottoes, nonpareils, rock candies, etc., according to fancy. If for cakes which are flat, the icing is equally spread over them with a spatula, and should not be so thin as for the high shaped cake, which cannot be spread so well with a knife. Coats of arms and other emblematical devices are often put on cakes, in which case the icing should be allowed to harden; after which trace the pattern with a pencil dipped in gum water, and gild it with gold and silver leaf, or Dutch metal. The icing is sometimes coloured with the extract of cochineal, lake or carmine, gamboge, etc. by taking a little of the colour and a spoonful of syrup, and pounding them in a small marble, or glass mortar, and mixing it with the icing. Cakes are also ornamented with gum paste in flowers, festoons, trophies, etc., etc. The paste may also be coloured in like manner. The moulds for gum paste, unless very finely cut, do not show so well. A board of various figures, such as leaves, flowers, trophies, etc. will cost about 3L. The

cakes usually ornamented are diet loaves, and formed in a great variety of shapes, as domes, obelisks, steeples, etc.

Such cake decoration was clearly an important step, but it was not at this stage directed to bride cakes and it was still a long way from any distinctive style of decoration for them. Indeed, their earliest differentiation in this respect was certainly an absence of decoration. A London publication of 1812 explains that the 'Bride or Christening Cake' 'is generally iced over like a Twelfth cake, when taken out of the oven; but without having any ornament whatever on the top, as it should appear of a delicate plain white'. He notes also that cochineal might be used for colouring a Twelfth cake (Macdonald 1812: 289–90, 300; cf. Kitchiner 1823: 443).

The earliest recorded departure from this pattern occurred in Scotland. The learned Mrs Johnstone of Edinburgh, 'Meg Dods' as was noted in the preceding chapter, offered instructions, beginning in her edition of 1833, 'To ice or frost a Bride's-cake, or very large Plum-Cake'. A royal icing is described, without any mention of an almond layer, but it is her recommendation on colour which is striking: the icing 'may be tinged with the juice of strawberries or currants, or with prepared cochineal. For a Bride's-cake confectioners use lake or cochineal ... Lemon-juice well beat with the sugar and white of eggs will make a white icing. No other *white* icing is admissible, yet vile ingredients are sometimes used' (Dods 1833 edn: 368–9). At the same time as this particular cake had gone pink, she notes also the use of wedding-related decorations, though not yet on cakes. On Bride's Pies, an alternative discussed in Chapter 4 above, 'appropriate ornaments and devices, as Cupids, turtles, torches, flames, darts, and other emblematic devices of this kind' (Dods 1833: 321–2) would be used. By her later editions these ornaments were clearly being used on cakes too, since she adds for further identification that they are 'of the wedding-cake kind' (Dods 1870 edn: 428).

The coloured cake was not to survive, however; it may never have appeared elsewhere at all. Even the symbolism of the decoration was perhaps a touch too ardent to survive long into the Victorian era, but by the mid-century decoration of other kinds was certainly coming in. For Queen Victoria's own wedding to Prince Albert in 1840 we have a description of the decoration of her cake which makes it sound more like a grand, serious and artistic Twelfth cake than the kind of thing later to emerge (Henisch 1984). It was a large single cake.

On the top was a device of Britannia blessing the bride and bridegroom, who are dressed, somewhat incongruously, in the costume of ancient Rome. At the foot of the bridegroom was the figure of a dog, intended to denote fidelity; at the feet of the Queen a pair of turtle doves. A host of gamboling Cupids, one of them registering the marriage in a book, and bouquets of white flowers tied with true-lovers' knots, completed the decoration. [4]

(Hindley 1878: 354)

It can be inferred that these devices were coloured and were displayed on white icing. As an inventory and exemplar of the wedding symbolism officially approved at the time the cake was and remains impressive (cf. Doyle 1850).

This marriage was, however, to support new and more sophisticated continental influences. Francatelli, already encountered, with his *The Royal English and Foreign Confectioner* (1862) represents the future mainstream. Though English by birth, he was a pupil of the great carême in France. As frontispiece for his book he displays a coloured illustration of a bride or wedding cake. This is still a single cake, though it is raised on an elaborate silver stand. He gives instruction for the preparation of such a cake: when the icing

has become hard, decorate it with royal icing piped on the top and sides, in tasteful ornamental designs; using also some buds and flowers, and wreaths of artificial orange flower blossoms, to be intermixed with the other mode of decoration. The whole of the ornamentation of a wedding cake must be white, with the exception of a wreath of blush roses.[5]

(Francatelli 1862: 99–100)

He describes the illustrated cake itself as 'surmounted with a floral fountain and a cupid', but this is scarcely an adequate description of what is shown. The 'floral fountain' looks like a miniature treetrunk entwined with white, presumably artificial, bell-shaped flowers and foliage. These are mounted in such a way as to fall downwards and outwards. Atop the tree sits the cupid, angel-like, amidst more flowers and birds. The whole appears to be covered in a white veiling material, though no comment on this is made. The stand is rather higher than the thickness of the cake itself, the 'floral fountain' at least as tall as cake and stand together.

Several features to be discussed in later sections are relevant here, its new tall shape, the extension of whiteness into the decorations, and, though they remain relatively naturalistic, a perceptible lessening of both their range and their representational nature. This latter had been strong in the Twelfth-cake tradition and even in the Queen's own cake.

Now a floral inclination is very apparent. But it is the mention of piping here – even though it is not apparent in the illustration – which has perhaps the greatest significance for the style of decoration which was about to develop. Piping was to take a generation to establish itself but was eventually to become a characteristic and essential feature of the wedding cake.

PIPING: 'A NEW ART FORM'

Piping is said to have been invented in the establishment of a certain M. Lorsa, a confectioner in Bordeaux (Vanaise 1928: 26). The story is that an unnamed apprentice one day cut off the point of a paper poke in which sweets were sold in the shop and, filling it with left-over meringue mixture, wrote his name with it on the work bench. M. Lorsa, finding him, at first was cross but quickly realised the possibilities. Filling the poke with royal icing, used at the time for marchpanes, he was quickly practising: 'au bout de quelques semaines il décorait parfaitement.' By 1842 potentials and techniques had been developed to such an extent that one of the employees in the same establishment was able to produce a piped model of Bordeaux cathedral, the very first 'grande pièce au cornet'.

The technology was refined by the manufacture of small metal funnels to fit into the bottom of a piping bag. These allowed particular shapes, soon numerous and fanciful, to be given to the icing extruded. It seems to have been another twenty years before piping began to be disseminated at all widely in Britain. Francatelli explained the process:

Icing Sugar for Ornamental Piping
Icing sugar is composed of the finest possible sifted loaf sugar, mixed or worked into a soft paste with whites of eggs and lemon juice. This kind of icing may be flavoured with different kinds of essences, or left plain, according to fancy. It is used for sheathing or covering wedding cakes, twelfth cakes, and a variety of other cakes, and for general ornamentation.

Instructions for the Use of Royal Icing
It is necessary to procure a variety of diminutive tin funnel-like cones (at Adams', 57, Haymarket, St. James'). The pointed ends of these are open, and are so contrived as to enable you, by their assistance, to produce every imaginable design of ornament ... it requires a knowledge of drawing, good taste, and practice, to produce a variety of neat or elegant designs of ornamentation, but you must not be deterred from trying your hand on account of these difficulties; for,

you must remember, that industry and perseverance overcome all obstacles.

(Francatelli 1862: 80–1)

Jeanes, offering rather the same explanation the year before, had noted that the 'small pipers or tubes' came 'principally from France, and are in sets of about twenty-five different patterns' (1861: 206).

Mrs Beeton's first picture of a wedding cake, in more informative colour than Francatelli's, was published in her *Every-day Cookery* (1872). It shows a neater and simpler cake, though large (20lbs). It was covered all over with smooth white icing and with white sugar ornamentation limited to a continuous line of small roses around the top edge. These may have been piped but may also, like Mrs Frazer's, have been applied sugarpaste. Around the side below this was a band of large red roses with green leaves, certainly applied, rather less naturalistic than Francatelli's and either of paste or fabric. The top of the cake was flat and plain, with an ornate white vase in which was a small arrangement of red roses, repeating the decoration of the sides, together with a white flower and foliage.

The scarcely visible, or indeed invisible, piping in these early illustrations was, as has been noted, the forerunner of great things to come. It made possible the development of the distinctive wedding-cake style of elaborate, highly repetitive and formal iced decoration. It was not perhaps a pre-requisite for the preoccupation with whiteness which developed, but it certainly made it possible to satisfy purists demanding a uniformity of shade by using the same icing for surface and for decoration. Piping also allowed striking effects to be produced, requiring expertise indeed but quickly and relatively cheaply, hence encouraging the production of decorated cakes on a larger scale for a less exclusive market. At the Universal Cookery and Food Exhibition, held in London in 1888, a commercial display, three categories of wedding cake were specified. There were elaborate cakes at eight and five guineas in one class – these would have used extravagant sugarpaste mouldings – and in another 'A two-guinea bride-cake, iced and piped by hand only'.

Enthusiasm for the new form eventually burgeoned too, though not without controversy. Robert Wells, a confectioner and author with strong feelings for naturalism and national identity – and affronted by the use of so foreign a plant as orange blossom – vigorously attacked the new style.

By nondescript decoration we mean the extraordinary shapes that some people put on cakes by means of pipes. We may call them dots,

or drops, or festoons, or curves, or whatever you like; but what are
they? what do they represent? Can any man, looking at them say that
is 'such a thing', and this is 'such a plant'? No, they are utterly
meaningless, and therefore senseless.[6]

(Wells 1890: 5)

Herr Willy responded with scorn in two editions of an equally vigorous
and opinionated book (1891). He had a school of piping and
ornamentation in London and had won a medal at the exhibition of
1888. His book publicised both his art and his school. This and works of
Richard Gommez (1895, 1896, 1899), a prolific author who also had a
school in London, display the trend, marked at the time, towards
regarding piping as a new medium for the production of Art. An
ever-increasing range of forms and styles, some transcending the normal
interests of confectioners, were being attempted and publicised. Of
more direct relevance to the wedding cake was the work of Ernest
Schülbé, a specialist in net and string work in icing, who established an
influential style which continued to be associated with his name. He
operated rather similarly in Manchester, with a 'Confectioner's School
of Art', and published a series of photographs of his often dazzling
designs in *Cake Decoration* (1898). A profusion of books on cakes and
their decoration had indeed begun to pour out.

Though the principles of piping could of course be applied to any
cake, and even to other foods altogether, the chief focus was on
the efflorescing wedding cake. Increasingly heavy and elaborate
encrustation developed, and other techniques were established; there
was Schülbé's net and string work, and also the piping of lacy and
lattice-work panels separately, for subsequent attachment and piping
into increasingly fantastic overall designs. For those in the trade who
had not yet managed to acquire the piping skills for themselves, Herr
Willy was offering in 1892 'piped tops', in sizes between 6 and 9 inches,
at prices ranging from 3s. to 4s. 6d. (see Figure 2). These, of typical heavily
encrusted style, were to be set on an otherwise undecorated cake. The
problem of matching with the sides was to be solved by hiding these with
a silver band and white frill. Such a solution could only be temporary and
makeshift though. Piping swept on and rapidly became the norm.

By the beginning of the new century the main exhibition class (4) was
for cakes decorated exclusively by piping; purists might judge the old-
style sugarpaste ornaments inappropriate because they were unlikely to
provide an exact match either in whiteness or style with the piped
decoration which had by then become the hallmark of the wedding cake
(Lewis & Bromley 1903: 19). An extra class. '4A Optional Decoration',

Figure 2 Advertisements in *The British Baker* (1893)

did however give room for continuing the tradition of cast sugarpaste architecture and sculpture from the previous century. Within the sphere of piped decoration, movements of fashion and even regional variations were becoming apparent. A lacy and almost organic style, lighter but highly complex, was displayed by practitioners from the south of England on specialised exhibition pieces. Schülbé's more formal style exploiting the possibilities of net work was prominent on somewhat more commercial cakes, and there were separate Scottish confectionery classes which included two for wedding cakes. These latter tended to be distinct again, more delicate and restrained in their decoration, or as a critic put it, 'severe, but classically beautiful' (Harris 1903: 60).

This was a period of remarkable excitement and experimentation in the confectionery trade generally. There was a sense of progress and expansion both artistic and commercial. New lines were being tried and sometimes established: an additional plain Groom's Cake was imported from the United States (Cordon Bleu 1893: 587; *BB* 1897: 68; see p. 80 above); there were Bridal Tartlets (Vine 1894: 68); and later Bridesmaid Cakes, also from America, and Betrothal Cakes, invented from scratch, both appeared with their own exhibition classes (Harris 1903: 23–4; Lewis & Bromley 1903: 55). But the wedding cake was the focus of enthusiasm and the pinnacle of confectionery achievement. In connection with it, direct commercial considerations might be transcended; hours of dedicated labour were put into the development and execution of magnificent specimens the only destination of which could be the exhibition or the shop window. The ferment of the period finally established that the wedding cake was an iced and normally a commercial product. In the 1870s and no doubt still later, amongst 'the cottage classes' even in the south of England this had not yet been so (Grey 1935: 156).[7]

7 The rise of the Victorian cake and its successors

Until the second half of the nineteenth century, there is no evidence that bride cakes were in shape different to any other kind of cake. They were inclined to be large but were otherwise the same as any other plum cake, that is to say round because they were baked in a hoop, and with a more or less flat top. Change occurred not by any dramatic invention or any sudden adoption of the three-tier edifice which was to become standard in the twentieth century. It was a matter of exceptional cakes and experimentation, with commercial interests again well to the fore. There was a gradual shift in expectations, from a single though large cake, to a large cake which might have more than one tier, and then to the three tiers. At the same time, 'bride cake' was largely replaced as the only regular term in use by 'wedding cake'.

PIÈCES MONTÉES

The change has its origins in an uprearing and elaboration of dishes and table decorations generally, in the first half of the nineteenth century. Carême in France had led a renewed fascination with pièces montées and a more general interest in the impressive presentation of food (Carême 1828; Mennell 1985: 144–50). In England, Alexis Soyer was a notable innovator and promulgator of new, lavish styles. Though French, he became one of the characters of Victorian England, head cook of the Reform Club in London, designer of banquets and writer on food. He presented his ideas enthusiastically in his books, notably *The Gastronomic Regenerator* (1846) and *The Pantropheon* (1853). In confectionery, Jarrin, who had worked in Paris and had even prepared celebration pièces montées for Napoleon, brought his talents to England and set up shop in Bond Street, London.[1] He published *The Italian Confectioner* in 1820, and this continued through three further editions up to 1844. Francatelli, born in London to Italian parents but apprenticed to Carême in Paris, maître d'hôtel to the Queen, has already been cited for his *Royal English and Foreign Confectioner* (1862).

Such men made the direct links in the highest reaches of society and for the most lavish catering. Table settings for grand occasions were given a strong vertical dimension. Food was raised on stands of one kind or another; there were tall vases of flowers and the stands for food even had flower arrangements placed on top of them; foods themselves were piled up or made in moulds to raise them like miniature castles; and there were extraordinary, towering constructions and sculptures in sugarpaste for the really grand event. Much of this was consciously architectural and paralleled the promiscuous antiquarianism of Victorian architecture, calling on the great past, be it Renaissance, Gothic or Classical, even Egyptian or, from the Empire, Indian (cf. *Art-Journal* 1851; Jones 1856). It would be by turns grand, picturesque and romantic. There were echoes here going back to medieval banquets and their subtleties, but more directly to the tradition of grand trionfi di tavola or pièces montées as it had developed on the Continent.

At a less exalted level too, the fashion for upstanding food spread widely. Tall moulds were used not just for jellied dishes; cakes were to be baked and puddings boiled in them also. The old-fashioned, round Christmas pudding boiled in a cloth was to be transformed to what looks to modern eyes like a black sandcastle. The movement was not new but in full flood when Mrs Beeton produced her *Every-day Cookery and Housekeeping Book* in 1872, designed to appeal to a less affluent market than her classic of eight years before. It contained the beautiful coloured plate which includes the wedding cake already referred to, but it also displays an array of strikingly upstanding cakes, puddings and desserts of various kinds.

ROYAL WEDDINGS AND THE HIGH RISING CAKE

For the grandest of official pastry and confectionery with its profusion of sugar architecture and sculpture, the continental pièces montées provided a very direct inspiration. The period is vividly expressed and copiously illustrated in *The Royal Book of Pastry and Confectionery* (1874), translated and adapted from his father's French work by Alphonse Gouffé, Head Pastry Cook to Her Majesty the Queen. Though this book does not notice wedding cakes, the movement received striking expression at the royal weddings of the period, those of Queen Victoria's children.

The Queen herself, at her wedding in 1840 to Prince Albert, had had 'a great beast of a plum-cake' which was nevertheless round and single:

'It weighed 300 pounds, was three yards in circumference, and fourteen inches in depth' (Hindley 1878: 354). It was made by Messrs Gunter and Waud in London and was to be backed up 'by a hundred others of a more decent size, which are to be distributed among her majesty's friends' (Doyle 1885: 12–13). It created a sensation in the capital. Eighteen years later however, times had changed. Again there was enormous popular interest, this time for the wedding of the young Princess Royal. For her there was a cake of the shape to which all such cakes would eventually aspire. The model had in fact appeared in the Great Exhibition in London of 1851. There, Gunter's firm had exhibited an all-purpose 'ornamental cake' of the new kind, designed by 'a clever Italian artist, M. Conté' (*Art-Journal* 1851: 81). It was a model to be followed, and intensively publicised, in the official cakes for each of her younger siblings in turn. Above a large circular base rose 'tiers', or 'compartments' as they were sometimes called in the earlier years, of declining diameter. Such cakes were between 5 and 7 feet high, and 2½ to 3 feet in diameter at the base. The tiers were not however separate cakes; only the base was of cake mixture, the upper tiers being entirely of sugar.

The first of the series in 1858 set the pattern. *The Illustrated London News* published a picture of it, as it was to do with most of the subsequent royal cakes, and an account of it was apparently communicated to the press, to be published with slight variations around the country.

THE ROYAL WEDDING CAKE

The wedding-cake was between six and seven feet high and was divided from the base to the top into three compartments, all in white.[2] The upper part was formed of a dome of open work, on which rested a crown. Eight columns on a circular plinth supported the dome and enclosed an altar, upon which stood two Cupids holding a medallion, having the profile of the Princess Royal on one side, and that of Prince Frederick William of Prussia on the other. Festoons as jasmine [sic] were suspended from the capitals of the columns, and busts of the Queen, the Prince Consort, the Prince of Prussia, and the Princess of Prussia were placed on four equidistant bases, projecting from the plinth. The middle portion contained niches in which were a number [4] of statues, including those of Innocence and Wisdom. These statues were separated by broad buttresses of an ornamental character, the upper parts decorated with festoons of orange blossoms and silver leaves. The side of the cake itself displayed the arms of Great Britain and Prussia, placed alternately on panels of white satin, and between each coat of arms was a medallion of the Princess Royal and Prince Frederick William encircled by orange blossoms, and surmounted by an imperial crown. Rows of pearls bordered each division of the cake, which was made by M. Pagniez, Her Majesty's confectioner. The cake was divided into a certain number of portions or slices, and each portion was decorated with a medallion of the royal bride and bridegroom.[3]

(*CC* 30 January 1858: 3)

According, however, to the *ILN* of 6 February following, it was M. Jules Le Blond who designed the cake. It was 'executed by him, with the assistance of M. Constant Pagnier, her Majesty's second confectioner'. This cake thus gained wide attention at the time; it was still remembered when Marchant came to write his history of wedding cakes and other wedding customs twenty years later.

Besides the official cakes which followed this pattern, at each royal wedding there was a second cake which responded more in its form to the development of wedding cakes in society at large. For that first wedding, it is only recorded that the second cake was by Mr Hankinson, 'English confectioner to her Majesty'. At the next wedding, of Princess Alice in 1862, there was 'a large cake made for the special use of her Majesty herself and the Royal Family' (*CC* 12 July 1862: 7). This cake was by Mr R. Bolland, a confectioner in Chester in the north of England.[4] He appears to have replaced Mr Hankinson but further details of the cake have not survived. At this wedding, which was rather small-scale and private, there was great emphasis on the distribution both of whole cakes and 4lb chunks of cake along royal and official channels. All these were provided by William Jeanes's firm, Gunter's of Berkeley Square, London.

A description is available, however, for the second cake at the Prince of Wales' wedding in the following year:

It weighed about 80lbs, and formed an octagon, covered with white satin, each side displaying alternatively medallions of the Prince of Wales, the arms of Great Britain, medallions of Princess Alexandra [the bride], and the arms of Denmark [from which she came]. The cornice was formed of large pearls. The cake was decorated with orange-blossom and jasmine, and the top was surmounted by a vase filled with a jasmine bouquet'.

(*ILN* 21 March 1863: 311, col. 3)

This cake was not, that is to say, like a modern wedding cake in shape. It was still, in the form prevailing at the time, a monstrous version of the single cake with a vase of flowers on top.[5]

A detailed description is available of the Bolland cake for the wedding of Princess Louise eight years later. By then, two tiers of cake with a third sugar tier above had become appropriate.

> It was made in three tiers, placed on a gold stand, weighing about 2 cwt, and measuring at the base of the lower cake two feet in diameter, and in height nearly five feet. The gold plateau had the royal arms on, at four equal distances, with cupids and flowers. The lower tier was ornamented with blue panels, baskets of flowers, fruit, and love birds between a scroll leaf, with medallions, containing likenesses of the Marquis of Lorne and the Princess Louise, with their respective coronets above each. The second tier was festooned with the rose, shamrock, and thistle. The third tier was entirely of net work, presenting a very light appearance, with cornucopias and shields, on which were the monograms of the bride and bridegroom. The whole was surmounted by a handsome vase of flowers, with silk banners edged with silver fringe, containing the armorial bearings of the Princess and of the Marquis. Each tier of the cake was bordered with trellise [sic] work studded with pearls.
>
> (*CC* 23 March 1871: 2)

Mrs Beeton's coloured plate of the same period is striking evidence that tiering was not yet generally established. The wedding cake illustrated is conspicuous by its simplicity. It is a round, hoop-baked cake with a flat top. It contrasts markedly with the upstanding chocolate and sponge cakes displayed on the same plate and particularly with a magnificent three-tiered gâteau. If the hint here can be taken, it may be suggested that the wedding cake itself was slow, as compared with other dishes, in developing upwards. Baking so large a cake was already technically more difficult. Mrs Raffald's warning against baking in pot or tin will be recalled. Francatelli (1862: 295), writing for the trade, suggested baking a large cake in four segments which could then be fitted together before the icing was applied, and Haldane (1883: 154), with the same problem in mind, recommended putting a pipe or funnel, made either of stiff paper or tin, into its centre. Subsequently, Lizzie Heritage (1894: 1015), writing for the home baker, noted that 'Unless the oven is very reliable, it will be better to send the cake to a baker's oven'. To bake anything so large in a mould was therefore impractical.

The first recourse for reaching high with such a cake was, as has been seen, sugarpaste architecture. This would, however, have been available only in the wealthiest reaches of society. Tall, silver stands were another possibility (*ILN* 1847: 249). Vases and flowers would have been more widely available: Lizzie Heritage suggested hiring a vase of flowers, presumably artificial, from a confectioner 'when a more elaborate cake is wanted' (Heritage 1894: 1015). But it was piling cakes one on another that was to be the real solution to the problem of making cakes rise impressively without recourse to sugarwork of a kind to be prohibitively expensive for almost everyone. The arrival of piping, discussed above, chiefly in the last decade or so of the century, meant that cakes baked separately but piled one on another could be elaborately but relatively cheaply encrusted with icing to make a single impressive structure.

Royal weddings continued to mark the progress. When Prince Leopold was married in 1882, there were three tiers and they were all cake (*CC* 22 April 1882: 8). Eleven years later when it was the turn of the Duke of York, afterwards King George V, there were four tiers of cake, with flowers on top. The wedding breakfast, with this cake prominently displayed on the table in front of the bride, appeared in *ILN* (10 July 1893) for all to see, and a model of it was subsequently displayed at the second Annual Confectioners and Bakers Exhibition held in London in September of the following year (*BB* 1894: 80).[6]

THE TRADE AND THE THREE-TIER STANDARD

The construction of such cakes was a skill for professionals, and indeed only at the top end of the baking and confectionery market. The tiered wedding cake was to become the flagship of the upper reaches of a burgeoning trade.[7] Leading firms competed by means of it at the series of culinary trade exhibitions which began in London in 1885 (Mennell 1985: 172). Standards were quickly propelled upwards and experiment was stimulated. The new style of cake has to be seen in this context as above all a commercial opportunity. Its subsequent spread throughout society was possible only in the form of a commercially produced commodity. Few ordinary people have ever had the capacity to bake at home on such a scale, let alone to provide the polished and regular style of decoration which set the standard.

Price, however, was the problem. In the 1880s commercial wedding cakes were available at from 10s. 6d. upwards (Haldane 1883: 153). Even this put them beyond the reach of many, and beyond the range therefore of the mass of small retail bakers and confectioners who catered for the less affluent. Skuse's *Complete Confectioner*, which was their guide, in repeated editions from 1879 onwards[8] was oblivious to wedding cakes, indeed to special-occasion cakes of any kind. Herr Willy writes: 'Orders for bride-cakes, the prices of which may be one or several pounds, more or less, are very scarce; many a small confectioner in all his life-long struggle never having a chance of such an order' (1891: 49). It was, however, to the trade that he and his piping school were chiefly catering, and he therefore pays attention to possibilities for expanding the market by reducing costs. He considers cheaper decorations for the top of cakes, and using a silver paper band to eliminate the time-consuming and therefore costly piping of their sides. Competition was a problem for the trade; he notes also that the basic price of bride cake in London was, at 1s. 6d. a pound, so low – it could be bought in pieces by weight, as well as in the form of whole cakes – that firms there needed to economise on the mixture they used for almond paste and on the thickness they applied. Elsewhere in the country, as perhaps at Bolland's establishment in Chester, prices of 2s. 6d. or even 3s. a pound gave scope for a better product.

By this kind of adaptation the purchase of wedding cakes was clearly spreading fast. A French observer noted the range of prices available, to suit all pockets 'depuis celle du plus humble citoyen justqu'à celle du Lord richissme' (Suzanne 1894: 232–4). The idea of a tiered cake was well established too. A commercial standard had already been set up by the 1888 Exhibition: a 36lb cake in class 5.2 would have had three tiers, a 30lb two, and both were far grander, as the prices indicate, than the relatively simple two-guinea bride cake. Even amongst the tiered, not all were quite what they seemed however. Gommez (1895: 97) comments on a photograph of an apparently three-tiered cake that the bottom tier was a dummy: 'This custom is becoming very fashionable amongst those who desire a large looking cake and at the same time only a small amount of cake.' But the expansion of sales in less affluent reaches of society had to be by means of cakes which, paying attention to Herr Willy, were no more than small and simple tokens of the grand, tiered edifices. Recipes appeared for cakes which could be sold at as little as 1s. per lb (Gommez 1896: 21). By 1903 a practical handbook for confectioners was offering instructions for single cakes to be sold at as little as 7s. 6d., rising to 21s. according to size. When authors did offer instructions for tiered cakes, these sometimes related explicitly to dummies for display in confectioners' windows and at exhibitions rather than to cakes for selling (Cox 1903).

What had not yet been altogether established, however, was the three-tiered standard which was subsequently to become part of the defining conventions of the wedding cake. The exhibition classes shifted from specifying weight and price to being based on the number of tiers, either three (class 4) or two (class 5) and usually contrasting by this means with all other cake classes except for a two-tier Golden Wedding cake. In these years the same leading names in cake decoration tended to win both the wedding-cake classes. The trade was, that is to say, encouraging the association of this particular cake with multiple tiers generally, but there were already clear pointers to a coming focus on three. The separate Scottish scheme of classes contained only a three-tier category (Harris 1903; Lewis & Bromley 1903). Mrs Beeton's famous *Book of Household Management* caught up with tiering in its 1906 edition. This included a new series of photographs of the stages in preparing dishes. One showed a relatively simple two-tier cake in preparation, with instructions at the foot of the plate for icing and piping. The main text still showed no recognition that wedding cakes were anything other than large iced cakes. The three-tier standard was only gradually established therefore. As late as 1968 the brochure of Fortnum & Mason, a highly traditional London store, displaying eight different models of cake included only two with three tiers; four had two and there were two singles.

SEPARATING THE TIERS

The relationship between the tiers was a matter for development too. At the beginning of the century it was generally still a matter of piling one cake directly on another and then decorating overall. There might be a pattern repeating from tier to tier but it was equally possible to use the entire structure for a single complex design varying in its forms from top to bottom. A major new development was however beginning. Richard Gommez's book of advanced piping and cake decoration (1899: 48–9) shows a drawing of an extraordinary three-tier cake with, most unusually, a title, *Goddess of Plenty*. It shows a peculiar range of assorted decorative devices, but its striking feature – at least with the benefit of hindsight – is that its upper tiers are raised above one another. He writes:

> The different tiers are raised in this cake by pieces of piped wood, leaving a space of 3 ins. between each tier. [There are four supports at each level, set to slope inward at an angle of about 45 degrees.] I need hardly add that the pieces of wood supporting the tiers may (as in this case) be cut from a broom-handle, and must be of one equal length. Also that a board is put under each cake to prevent the supports piercing the cake and thus jeopardising its equilibrium; the supports may be piped in pale green, which shows through the mass of white very effectively and prettily.

At the Tenth International Exhibition held in London in 1902, new possibilities of this kind were becoming clearly visible. The winning three-tier cakes of class 4 had their upper tiers raised by concealed blocks to give them extra height whilst retaining the established solid-mounted look, but there were also cakes appearing with pillars of the style subsequently to become standard. Though it did not win a prize, a commentator noted and illustrated 'A new form cake – a very pretty form indeed – preserved in each tier' (Harris 1903: 8–9). Each tier was in shape not round but a square superimposed on a circle, giving alternating pointed projections and curves around its circumference. Of direct relevance here however were the four squat pillars between bottom and middle and middle and top tiers. These did not, however, meet the approval of the critical commentator: they were felt not to match the icing, being bluish, and they introduced 'a jarring note'. Pillars were rather more evident in the Scottish section. The third-prize winner was a cake from Edinburgh in which 'The different tiers are supported on frames made of plain silvered discs, with plain, straight silver pillars between'. These he thought 'plain even unto homeliness' (Harris 1903: 63). A Highly Commended cake used straightforward pillars, four above and six below, and there were more obviously experimental versions too, with various combinations of pillars, frames and solid mounting.

The direct source of such innovations is not far to seek. Class 4A for cakes in any style of decoration reached back to the traditions represented by the royal cakes of the previous century but at the same time allowed more scope for experimentation. Influenced by what had happened in the mainstream, such cakes now needed to incorporate at least three solid cakes into their architectural and sculptural fantasies. This meant raising them and had produced experimentation as to practicable and elegant means of doing so. One solution was a 'drum', i.e. a single large central support; another, highly eccentric and shown hors concours by Cox's firm in Hastings, had the separate cakes 'suspended in mid-air by having the trunk of a small tree pushed through them all' (Harris 1903: 57–8); but the use of pillars was perhaps the most obvious. Pillars, or columns, had been a prominent feature of the sugar architecture both before and after cakes themselves began to be piled up. The bottom two tiers of Prince Leopold's cake, referred to above, were ringed with columns supporting decorative features at the level of the tier above. Columns or pillars had also appeared supporting the cakes themselves as parts of elaborate cake stands. A picture exists of a single-tier model from as early as 1847 (*ILN* 1847: 248), and a striking double-tier one is shown in the frontispiece to a volume of *The Modern Baker, Confectioner and Caterer* (Kirkland 1909). Against this background, it was but a small step to move pillars into the structure of 'the cake' itself.

Solid mounting, without the use of pillars, took time to disappear. Up to the early 1930s, both styles might still be found in brochures, e.g. of the Glasgow Co-operative Bakers, but by the middle of the decade it had gone.[9] A. R. Daniel's *Up-to-date Confectionery*, still publishing in the 1970s but dating originally from 1936, could take pillars for granted. The three-tier model was also by then well established. A major West of Scotland wedding-cake baker and caterer was, in the early 1930s, categorising their cakes as 'bottom', 'middle' and 'top', despite the fact that, of those they actually sold, never more than a quarter boasted the full three tiers. By far the commonest order was for two tiers.

Pillars presented a new technical problem, namely how to prevent them sinking into the cake below. This and the need to cater to the three-tier standard meant that amateur cake-making became that much harder again: icing too hard to be cut and sinking pillars remain the two hazards of home-prepared wedding cakes well known to caterers today. One device already referred to above met the problem by means of 'silver or silver-plated combined pillars and supports'. Thin silver boards or discs were the main possibility. 'In either case a very great weight can be supported without difficulty' (Daniel 1978: 420).

Pillars also went with other significant changes, grounded in movements of taste. The cake became a lighter-seeming edifice. There were the less heavily encrusted styles of piping already noted in 1902, and the number and variety of ideas applied to a single cake were limited by treating each of the tiers identically. Each would be decorated to repeat on a smaller scale the design of the one below it. This produced what may be called the Edwardian cake. As the culmination of the separation of the tiers, it rapidly became a fundamental and long-lasting feature of the wedding-cake conception.

Until the 1930s almost all cakes were basically round, though this was another matter which had received attention in the innovative 1890s: at the Manchester Exhibition of 1896, there had been a class for three-tier wedding cakes 'in a new form, each tier to be of a different shape, but none of them to be circular' (*BB* 1896: 83). This proved too radical to be influential; the opposite assumption, that each tier would duplicate its fellows in shape as well as in decoration, was to become firmly established.

In the 1930s, however, novelty shapes as well as colours began to be introduced. Apart from square cakes which then appeared, it was the horseshoe which was sufficiently popular for tins for baking it in to begin to be manufactured (Nirvana 1946: 90). Joe Loss, a popular band leader married in 1938, had a single-tier, horseshoe cake with models of a band as well as a bride and groom arranged on it (*Good Housekeeping* 1989: 87). After the war the confectioner who had been writing under the pseudonym of Nirvana since the 1920s tried to popularise the heart shape. He attempted a symbolic link: 'it is certain that the heart does play an important part in the process of courtship and marriage, and for this reason alone a tangible pardon is due to the intrepid pioneer who ventures to apply the shape to commercial practice' (Nirvana 1951: 116). He notes that by then the square cake seemed to have come to stay, but his own pioneering had no striking success. More ambitiously even, Daniel's manual has over the years offered instructions for making a cake in the shape of a double heart, with the names of bride and groom piped on the top in birthday-cake style (1978: 410). It was not until the late 1980s that such radical departures began to find favour. One firm studied made this particular design for the first time ever in 1990.

Simpler shapes more suitable for tiering took hold earlier. By the beginning of the 1980s a range of possibilities was on offer, of which the hexagonal was probably the most successful, but many individual firms were still offering only round or square. The latter were the more popular and seemed at the time to be establishing themselves as the new norm. It began to be square cakes that new books of wedding etiquette would choose for their covers (e.g. Derraugh 1983) and magazine articles on wedding arrangements would illustrate. Square cakes were, it was always said, more convenient for cutting up.

By 1990, as we have seen, a revolution was occurring. Sugarpaste was once again in vogue, though it was now Australian 'plastic icing' that provided the alternative to royal icing, with the old style of sugarpaste confined to modelling. With it came a new emphasis on rounded and less regular shapes, readily draped with the new sugarpaste but more diffi- cult to cover smoothly with royal icing. The round cake itself received new impetus, once again rivalling the square, and the heart became a more practical and popular possibility. Hexagons and even octagons remained popular, and what was generally known as 'petal' shape – in fact the shape of a stylised open flower – was a new design with a strong appeal. Horseshoe, oval and diamond were other possibilities. Shape, from being a constant, had become a conspicuous dimension of choice.

COLOUR, TOP PIECES AND OTHER ORNAMENTATION

At least from the mid-eighteenth century onwards, achieving a white finish was, as has been seen, a clear consideration in icing cakes. The need to use the best and most highly refined sugar obtainable made of it an ultimate in cost and luxury (cf. Mintz 1985: 77–8, 87). There was therefore initially and for a long time no connection between this whiteness and any particular occasion for which the cake might be prepared. It was probably only towards the middle of the nineteenth century that matters began to change. Dods's and Francatelli's evidence cited above show that even the whiteness of the cake was not yet a matter to be taken for granted, but they also clearly show that such cakes were coming to be differentiated. This was happening against a background of proliferating types of cake, colours of icing, and styles of decoration. For long indeed, the absoluteness of the whiteness which was required remained variable. It was much less in Mrs Beeton's illustration of 1872 than it had been in Francatelli's ten years before, and neither were as overwhelmingly white as cakes were later to become.

An article in *The British Baker* for February 1887 on 'How to colour cakes' shows that new meanings had by then become firmly attached. It was protesting that the whiteness of wedding and christening cakes, 'which is so intimately associated with purity, is allowed to become horribly monotonous'.

> A leading London firm decorate theirs with real flowers and ferns; but they confine the colours to green, with perhaps a yellow petal or two of a lily, and, of course, white; but without doubt, in our eyes, they are far more artistic on colour grounds than most we have seen. Still, there is not enough warmth about them. Along with green maidenhair ferns – for these are the principal foliage plants they use – a few warm rose-tinted flowers might surely be introduced. In season, say, the wild rose; and, with all possible regard to the association of purity, there is as much purity in wild roses as in lilies. It is difficult to educate people out of a custom, especially if that custom be in connection with marriage ceremonies, and while confectioners should be careful not to suddenly shock the sensibilities of their customers, yet improvements may be gradually made. Among the beautiful fern cakes, one's eye looks with eager expectation for a bright truss or two of scarlet geranium. Some day it may be gratified. We would limit the trusses to two; and we do not believe any bride would object; nay, we feel sure the natural instinct for appreciating red amid green would prevail, and she would be gratified.

The anonymous author of this piece might almost have been describing Mrs Beeton's cake of only fifteen years before as his ideal. By the time he or she was writing, however, protest was in vain. Herr Willy was to note (1891: 51–2): 'Any kind of white or very dainty-coloured flowers, blossoms, buds, may be applied as decoration on bride-cakes.' There were new ones all the time 'but orange blossoms, snowdrops, camelias, water and other lilies, azaleas, daisies, stephanotis, white roses, etc., as known by everybody, have still the preference.' The dominantly white cake had become firmly established and ruled unchallenged until the inter-war period.

Colour then became possible again, as an exciting innovation. There could be colour in ornaments, in the piping and even in the basic icing. A West of Scotland baker and caterer specialising in weddings was offering pink cakes in the 1930s, though less than one in ten of the orders actually received varied from white in this way. Indeed, little impression was made and when cake decoration resumed after the war the accent was once more on whiteness (Nirvana 1946: 76; 1951: 89). In the 1960s it was possible again therefore to announce colour as the new innovation. A black and white cake created a stir when exhibited at an Olympia (London) exhibition in 1963 (Daniel 1978: 420). By the early 1980s even, though the West of Scotland firm had a cake business ten times as large as in the 1930s and was prepared to do any shade requested, as far as the base icing was concerned the proportion coloured had not greatly increased, though the possible colour range had (see p. 14 above). Even by 1990, a survey suggested that a majority of British cakes were still white but that other pale colours were perhaps at last making a larger impression. Different confectioners identified different favourites at the time, but ivory and cream led the field – with 'champagne' and 'pine' probably indicating something not very different – and with pink and peach, both very pale, well behind. Lemon and blue were mentioned. A Swansea confectioner, following the 1963 precedent, displayed black and white cakes in 1989–90. They drew no sales but plenty of attention, most of the comment being adverse: 'more like a funeral cake than a wedding one' (Margaret Kenna 1989, personal communication).

Any departure from white was consciously linked to the colours of bride's and bridesmaids' dresses (Nirvana 1951: 125). A bride wearing a variant of the standard white was likely to want, or to be advised to have, a cake with a base icing to match.[10] Piping might be of a different colour and was rather more likely to diverge from white. It was occasionally matched to the colour of bridesmaids' dresses, and further 'trimmings' were very commonly so.

Such further decoration of the cake has always been highly distinctive. The ideal of the late Victorian and Edwardian periods, on which the literature generated by the enthusiastic confectioners of the time concentrates, was of a cake relying for its effect entirely on its piped decoration. There was a strong purist streak here. The ornamentation was to be all of a piece, uniform in its whiteness, sheerly decorative and finished only with a flower arrangement on its top. In contrast to the sugarpaste style which it superseded, it eschewed representation and any overt symbolising. Though this ideal exerted a strong influence on the form and development of the British cake, it was too demanding to win universal acceptance. On the one hand, neither the purse of the customer nor the skills of many confectioners could rise immediately to the fulfilment of the ideal, on the other, there was always some demand for decoration which could be more directly related to the occasion. By the late 1880s there were specialist suppliers of attachable wedding-cake ornaments advertising their wares.

The vase to contain the flowers which were the established complement for the top of the cake was the focus for developments which infringed ideals least. Appropriate styles quickly appeared and were apparently supported even by the high priests of the trade. The best were made in white Parian ware, echoing both the whiteness and the texture of the cake's iced surface. They might be of simple, elegant shapes, but often they were more elaborate, typically incorporating cherubs in a move back to established symbols of love and marriage.

In Britain, flowers retained their dominance for the top of cakes.[11] At the earlier period there was often a sizeable vase with a substantial flower arrangement in it. This was sometimes referred to as the bride's bouquet; indeed it may sometimes have been the one she had carried at church earlier in the day. On a tall cake it would generally have trails of flowers descending on opposite sides: Willy noted that if there were more than one tier, 'some sprays hanging down the sides will appear effectual' (1891: 53). Wells, an opponent of the new orthodoxy, challenged the logic of making plants which were not creepers hang down in this way (1890: 3). Vase and flowers might well in such a scheme account for more than half the total height. With the introduction of pillars, this began to change. If there were still flowers, it would be no more than a spray in a small, elongated but plain vase, often in silver plate. The trails first retreated and then disappeared, removing any sense of the flowers embracing the cake and softening its hard outlines.

At an early stage, however, the use of artificial flowers began to change the range of possibilities. They might be delicately made in elaborate arrangements, designed to be kept and displayed as a souvenir of the wedding, often under a glass dome. But if the flowers were artificial they would not need a real flower vase for their display. The way was open for a variety of unified and more varied ornaments using flowers, near-flowers and other more directly symbolic objects. In the long run, as we have seen, bride and groom would become the leading motif. An advertisement in *The British Baker* of 1892 by a Scottish firm making a patent icing powder included a cake ornamented on top with such a bride and groom, a harbinger of an idea which was to run around the world in the mid-twentieth century.

The new unified ornaments might be mass produced and sold complete. It seems to have been the United States which made the pace here. There, by the turn of the century, ornaments of a much more representational and symbolic kind than were favoured for wedding cakes in Britain were being produced. Weaver (1988) illustrates a New York example advertised in 1899. An inverted horseshoe is mounted on an elaborately decorated pedestal. Upon the pedestal an anvil stands amongst flowers; a blacksmith forges two rings on it. He is framed by the horseshoe which carries the legend 'CONSTANCY'. 'GOOD LUCK' is partly visible behind the figure. The horseshoe is itself crowned and framed by flowers and foliage. Hueg (1901: 74) shows bride-and-groom designs, including one in which they stand in a similar horseshoe grotto with the legend 'GOOD LUCK'. Here, however, a swinging bell elaborately framed in flowers and foliage adds another tier on top. By the 1920s the bride and groom were firmly established and 'cewpies' had appeared too (Bauer 1924). Cewpies were child bride and groom figures, the name presumably indicating the original motivation, an amalgamation of cupids with a marrying couple. This was to prove a long-runner too: though origins and even the term had long been forgotten, the tradition crossed the Atlantic and was still in evidence in figures for cakes and in designs for wedding stationery in Britain in the 1980s.

There, however, wedding cakes remained strikingly formal. Though those planning London exhibitions in the late 1930s tried to move fashion on by requiring exhibitors to include in their designs some representation of 'the pursuit or calling of the bride or bridegroom' (Nirvana 1951: 11; cf. Hanneman 1978: 217), any wider response was very limited. Rarely has there been much beyond the colour, and that only occasional, to associate the cake with a particular couple or their particular wedding. Even the figures have always been generalised representations, a bride and groom not necessarily dressed in the same way as the marrying couple themselves, and even then this form of decoration has been looked on askance by many who have preferred to keep to flowers. Other ornaments of a symbolic nature have remained few and highly stylised: for a time early in the century, joined hands were popular; doves on metallic rings, either gold or silver, started early and never altogether disappeared, and silver or white slippers, cupids and horseshoes remained popular over a long period.

The major exceptions were banners and, in Scotland, favours. From the 1880s to the Second World War, and in some remote corners of

Scotland even to the present, silk or paper banners with the initials of the couple and the date of the wedding would be prepared and hung on sticks above or beside the cake. These began in the upper reaches of society. Princess Louise's cake of 1871, described above, displayed forerunners and, by 1880, Trollope was able to write in his novel *The Duke's Children* (Chapter 79) of the 'terrible tower of silver which now stands niddle-noddling with its appendages of flags and spears on the modern wedding breakfast-table'.[12] The banners became a means of identifying the cake with a particular couple and wedding, without breaching a tacit rule observed by all but the most aristocratic levels of society, the rule against including writing in the decoration on wedding cakes in the way common on cakes for other celebrations. Amongst the aristocracy, monograms and heraldry might continue, a conservative retention of pre-piping styles.

Favours were not quite so explicit. In the seventeenth century favours were usually knots of ribbon which were distributed to those whom it was desired to associate with the wedding and to honour (Gillis 1985: 61). There might be bridegroom's as well as bride's favours, in distinctive colours, which each side would give to its associates. As a practice this might be built into a small rite. From a wedding amongst the gentry of Edinburgh in 1704 there exists an account of such a development:

> The Brides favours were all sowed on her gown from tope to bottom and round the neck and sleeves. The moment the ceremony was performed, the whole company run to her and pulled off the favours: in an instant she was stripd of all of them. The next ceremony was the garter. . . .
>
> (Mure 1854: 264)

Here therefore, the bride's favours were associated with her person by being lightly tacked to her dress.

The subsequent history of favours in Scotland is not known but in England they continued to be distributed, at times at least and by more mundane methods. They were co-opted to the white wedding in the nineteenth century. They might be worn by all the male guests (Doyle 1850) or they might be used, like the ribbon on the wedding car today, to mark the horses and coaches and servants associated with a wedding. Late in the century they were being made of artificial flowers as well as white ribbon and were said to be indispensable for an English wedding (Sherwood 1884: 71). Subsequently they died out in England. In Scotland, however, they reappear in the record in the twentieth century attached to the cake. It is possible indeed that the apparent plainness and severity of Scottish exhibition cakes was the result of their use as a vehicle for favours. As the preoccupation with whiteness declined, these small confections of ribbons and artificial flowers, or tartan and heather for a self-consciously Scottish model, could become more colourful. They became an item to be chosen separately, to be matched to the bridesmaid's dress, attached to the cake, and then to be distributed at the end of the celebration (Charsley 1991: 172–3). They became, that is to say, a main way in which a standard cake would be personalised for the particular wedding.

Part III

Users, uses and meanings

8 Uses and their evolution

The Victorians' attempt to tell a unified story of the cake and its uses up to their own time was not entirely groundless, for one of our themes must be the way in which established practices suggest new possibilities. There is indeed a kind of evolution here, in which each stage is a starting point from which those coming to it afresh begin. Often they merely reproduce what they have found, but sometimes not. Sometimes circumstances make it impossible; sometimes it becomes for some people undesirable; sometimes a practical advantage in change is identified; and sometimes perhaps the spirit of creative experimentation which humanity at its best can display intervenes for no very clear reason at all. And whenever there is change and ideas of any kind are brought to bear on it they can hardly come from elsewhere than the experience of the people concerned. There is therefore another kind of continuity too, in which old possibilities are recycled in new forms. Though there is no single story of cultural change to be told, and the search for a single theory of cultural change must in the end prove fruitless, there are striking links and patterns always to be found. In this chapter cake-breaking and cake-cutting, the two major lines of development, and the way they have been linked by dreaming will be traced. The two will be seen to spring initially from different kinds of 'cake' and to parallel one another in their development. Other ways in which cakes have been used will emerge as the discussion proceeds.

CAKE-BREAKING

'Cake-breaking' is a term marooned and made surprising by movements of material culture which have been traced in earlier chapters. We have seen how the distinction between cake and bread was created, with cake, and particularly the wedding cake, becoming an object less and less suitable for breaking. But even if the cake to be broken is thought of as bread, the modern British loaf and the sliced form of it which has become such a fact of life do not encourage anyone formed by British culture to recognise something much more familiar here.[1] It is clear, however, that many forms of bread baked in the past would, like traditional French loaves even today, readily break. A small reminder only is needed that the expression 'the breaking of bread', or 'to break bread together', is familiar and is not even in origin metaphorical. It has acquired resonance in Christian cultures, with symbolic links created, as a part of the central Christian ritual, the mass. This has then been separated from its everyday practical context, again marooned by material and cultural change. Earlier 'cakes' for weddings would, like any others, have been destined for breaking in the normal course of events, to be shared out for eating.

Though it comes from a much later period, an account of the preparation of such cakes catches this earlier normality. Gregor (1881: 89) reports that in the north-east of Scotland there had been there a definite 'beuckin nicht' for making the 'bridal bread': 'In baking the cakes,[2] great care was taken with the first cake lest it should be broken – a broken cake portends unhappiness'; a cake broken, that is to say, before its proper time. Here the cakes – not one but several – were to be teamed up with the 'bridal ale', representing a secularised version of the last stage of the nuptial mass, persisting here three hundred years after the abolition of the mass at the Reformation.[3]

From the time of the earliest references to the practice in the seventeenth century however, there is little doubt that we are dealing not with a mere prelude to eating but with a breaking which has become a rite in itself, associating the cake directly with the bride. Later it becomes clear that this was achieved by breaking the cake over the bride's head; there is no reason to think that it was different on earlier occasions less explicitly described.

Whether we have to do here with a practice which had established itself in the preceding period and now came occasionally to be recorded, or with a campaign to install in Britain a practice thought to have the endorsement of antiquity, cannot be entirely clear. Herrick's poem, 'Julia's churching', from the first half of the seventeenth century, is perhaps the earliest source, and Herrick was an enthusiast for the classical world; it is difficult in his work to disentangle the classical model from the contemporary relevance.[4] Whether as ethnography or as a contribution to cultural propaganda his poem is indeed striking; it includes implied interpretation as well as the apparent documentation.

Julia is represented as returning from her re-entry to church after giving birth, as if from her wedding:

All Rites well ended, with faire Auspice come
(As to the breaking of a Bride-Cake) home:
Where ceremonious Hymen shall for thee
Provide a second Epithalamie.

The following verse then provides a moralising gloss on the first, including presumably 'the breaking of the Bride-cake', which makes explicit its sexual connotations.

She who keeps chastly to her husbands side
Is not for one, but every night his Bride:
And stealing still with love, and feare to bed,
Brings him not one, but many a Maiden-head.

Later in the century Aubrey (1881: 22, 181) refers to bridal cake-breaking, also linking the term 'bride-cake' to it, if somewhat inexplicitly, and connecting it with ancient Roman practice.

Such antiquarian concerns were very real in seventeenth century England, and they might also influence practice. 'Confarreation', the anglicised form of the Latin term for the marriage procedure thought to involve cake-breaking, was then occasionally used as a synonym for 'marriage' or 'wedding'. A letter of 1625 offering cautious counsel about an impending marriage ends: 'So, wishing you all conjugal Joy and a happy *Confarreation*, I rest – Your affectionate Cousin' (Howell 1890: 221). From the late sixteenth century there was also an enthusiasm for quoting classical epithalamies, or nuptial songs, and for writing new ones in English after classical models (e.g. Howell 1890: 129, as well as Herrick above). In so far as cakes were actually broken over heads, this may therefore have been at least encouraged, and perhaps even initiated, as an appropriate echo of what was taken to be classical custom.

It is certainly interesting in this context that the best known instance of cake-breaking in English literature, from the following century, is not presented as current practice but is again referred to ancient times. Here it is the ancient Britons to whom Smollett, in *The Expedition of Humphrey Clinker* (1771), attributes it. This book leads up to the triple wedding of three assorted couples, aspects of which receive detailed description. The church ceremony is the first major focus, and the participants' clothes for this are carefully described. There is no mention of any bride cake to be eaten then or at the dinner following. The second focus of interest is in what happens after dinner. Then each couple is treated in ways thought appropriate to their ages and status. As one couple 'were judged improper objects of mirth, Jack Wilson had resolved to execute some jokes on Lismahago, and, after supper, began to ply him with bumpers [i.e. toast glasses full to the brim], when the ladies had retired.' But he begged out of it.

> He was spared accordingly, and permitted to ascend the nuptial couch with all his senses about him. There he and his consort sat in state, like Satan and Cybele, while the benediction posset [a drink, made probably at this period of wine, egg yolks, sugar and spice, perhaps milk] was drunk; and a cake being broken over the head of Mrs Tabitha Lismahago, the fragments were distributed among the bystanders, according to the custom of the ancient Britons, on the supposition that every person who ate of this hallowed cake should that night have a vision of the man or woman whom Heaven designed should be his or her wedded mate.
>
> (Smollett 1771: 227–8)

There are always problems in inferring social practice from fiction. While authors necessarily produce texts from their own culture and time, they are more likely to present events that are in some way unusual, and therefore interesting to themselves and to their expected readers, than they are to describe the entirely usual. Here, clear evidence is provided that ideas of cake-breaking were around in the late eighteenth century, but the important implications are otherwise negative. It can be inferred from this account that no such practice was either general amongst likely readers of the book or even regarded as having been general in the recent past. Nor was anything of the kind thought to be in any way essential.

There is however other sporadic evidence of such practices from England at the period (Gillis 1985: 137–8), and from Scotland the evidence may even suggest something more generalised. The earliest Scottish report is not indeed of bread or cake of any kind, but the analogy is clear: at the beginning of the eighteenth century, Lady Grisell Baillie bought in Edinburgh for her daughters' marriages ribbon 'for the Garland that is brock over the Brids head', as well as 'Confections Plumcaks and Bisket from Mrs Fenton' (Scott-Moncrieff 1911: 115, 203–5, 217). It is tempting to see this as a modification, suitable for gentry who had already joined the plum cake class, of an earlier, more earthy cake-breaking. Smollett's reference to 'ancient Britons' may draw similarly on Scottish experience. He was born and brought up in the Vale of Leven at the south end of Loch Lomond. At its foot on the River Clyde lies Dumbarton, once the capital of the British kingdom of Strathclyde – his 'ancient Britons' perhaps. An almost guide-book tour of this area is featured in the book. It is again tempting to imagine that it was from his youth there that he remembered the cake-breaking which he now called into his narrative.

Certainly, from soon after Smollett was writing, cake-breaking is directly documented (weddings in Strathdearn, 1774–83, quoted by Grant 1961: 33). In parts of Scotland an oatcake or shortbread might be broken over the head of a bride as she entered a house after the marriage. This was often her entry into the groom's house where she would henceforth be living (as was indeed implied by Herrick's poem), but Gregor, a folklore researcher in the north-east of Scotland whose testimony has already been quoted, suggests a wider range of possibilities. It might be an oatmeal cake that was broken over her head. 'In later times a thin cake of "short-bread", called the bride-cake, was substituted for the oatmeal cake. It was distributed among the guests, who carefully preserved it, particularly the unmarried, who placed it below their pillows to "dream on".' (Gregor 1881: 92–3). From the South of Scotland, another writer has a more detailed and rather different procedure to report:

> as the newly-married wife enters her new home on returning from the kirk, one of the oldest inhabitants of the neighbourhood, who has been stationed on the threshold, throws a plateful of short-bread over her head, so that it falls outside. A scramble ensues, for it is deemed very fortunate to get a piece of the short-bread, and dreams of sweethearts attend its being placed under the pillow.
>
> (Henderson 1866: 22)

It might, however, be a more straightforward 'bread' that was used. Returning again to the North East:

> When passing over the threshold there was held over the bride's head a sieve containing bread and cheese, which were divided among the guests. They were sometimes scattered around her, when there was a rush made by the young folks to secure a piece. . . . In some districts, when the sieve was in the act of being placed over her head, or the bread broken, it was the bridegroom's duty to snatch her from below it. She was led straight to the hearth . . . [where her husband's mother who had welcomed her at the door would present her with tongs and broom, interpreted as making her a 'gueedwife', i.e. goodwife or mistress of the household].
>
> (Gregor 1881: 92–3)

For the fishing population, the same author provides a separate account, written this time in the present tense:

When the bride is entering her future home, two of her female friends meet her at the door, the one bearing a towel or napkin, and the other a dish filled with various kinds of bread. The towel or napkin is spread over her head, and the bread is then poured over her. It is gathered up by the children who have collected round the door. In former times the bride was then led up to the hearth. . . .

(Gregor 1881: 99)

There was sometimes a recognised day and name for this event, the infare. This was to be distinguished from the bridal which had preceded it, as in Joanna Baillie's song written in the early nineteenth century:

At bridal and infare, I braced me wi' pride,
The broose I hae won, and a kiss o' the bride'.

(Baillie 1851: 824)

The infare was the last stage of the celebrations, after the feasting and dancing were over. It might, hence, be the 'infar-cake' which was broken (Agrestis 1818; Napier 1879: 51; Rogers 1884: 117–18). A fragment of a poem quoted in a Glasgow wedding-cake brochure of the 1930s includes the line, 'Joes are spae'd [i.e. sweethearts are foretold] by th'Infar Cake'.

From the English side of the Borders of the early nineteenth century comes a further variant:

Bride-cake. The bridal party, after leaving the church, repair to a neighbouring inn, where a thin currant-cake, marked in squares, though not entirely cut through, is ready against the bride's arrival. Over her head is spread a clean linen napkin, the bride-groom standing behind the bride, breaks the cake over her head, which is thrown over her and scrambled for by the attendants.

(Carr 1828: 51)

Almost half a century later, in east Yorkshire the procedure had separated altogether from the bride. At her arrival 'at her father's door', pieces of cake on a plate would be flung from an upper window. What happened to the cake is lost sight of but the plate should break into as many pieces as possible (Henderson 1866: 21–2).

It is clear therefore that, though the evidence is very scattered, in parts of northern Britain cake-breaking took hold and had evolved locally into a variety of forms before it died out almost everywhere in the nineteenth century.[5] This variety is striking: pouring of already broken or cut-up pieces might have been substituted for breaking, undermining any directly sexual interpretation which might previously have been offered; if any pouring or breaking were to take place the bride in a daintier age could expect to be protected by a cloth over her head; bread and its common complement cheese might have been substituted for any kind of cake; the foodstuffs might be merely held above the bride's head, at first in token of the pouring or breaking, abandoned perhaps for reasons of hygiene; it might have become the groom's task to rescue his bride as if from a threat; and finally, there might still be a kind of pouring but one which had deserted the bride's person altogether, with attention shifting onto the fate of the plate. Though there is no commentary on any of this sequence in the literature, it is full of suggestion of the ways in which the development and differentiation of popular rites occur.

There is no single logic here. Van Gennep's theory of rites of passage may seem to provide the key to a part of it; it would be surprising if it did not, for what is occurring here is exactly the kind of transition which was central to his thinking. But as so often happens, the events are ambiguous. As long as something was being broken, it is tempting to interpret this as a separation. The woman is leaving behind either her single state or her liminal status as bride.[6] But pouring pieces over her does not suggest the same interpretations at all. Both however may be interpreted as liminal rites, especially as they appear to have occurred typically at the threshold of the house in which her new status was to be assumed. They are alike in being abnormal uses of food, uses indeed which at other times would be irresponsible and wasteful, the opposite of the careful control of food which would be the new 'gueedwife''s responsibility. They make therefore an admirable assertion of the abnormal state of the bride, already married but not yet inducted into her new role. Merely holding bread and cheese over her in a sieve, or rescuing her from the pouring, does not belong here at all, however.

In the absence of contemporary commentary it is impossible to say what they did ever represent to anybody, but it looks as if a different sense of the bride had intervened. She now needed, it may have been thought, to be protected from the messy results of the older practice, either by being covered with a cloth first, or by avoiding the pouring altogether. And once not only the breaking but even pouring had been abandoned, bread might suggest cheese; its even greater unsuitability for pouring would have become irrelevant. Evolving practices give scope for the application of new logics.

DREAMING AND DIVINATION

Old ideas may also be applied in new situations. Dreaming of a future spouse by sleeping with a piece of cake under one's pillow, with or without eating a piece of it too, has occurred, as has already been seen, in a variety of contexts, from the seventeenth century 'dumb cakes' (Aubrey 1881: 65) onwards to the present day. In the later eighteenth century and connected with the plum-cake style of bride cake – hence with more genteel sections of society – a new way of associating pieces of cake with the bride was developed. Whereas cake-breaking had been something done to the bride, the new practice was, with some initial ambiguity, something she would do. Little pieces of cake might be passed through the wedding ring. This is reported from a gentry wedding in Berkshire in 1770. It was recorded by the Rev. Stotherd Abdy, the officiating clergyman, who was staying in the house as one of the wedding party. After the ceremony:

> we all adjourned to the Drawing Room in order to insert the marriage in the Register. We then (as the morning was exceedingly fine & it was too early for dressing for the great appearance) walked round the garden, & thro' the Wilderness, after which we came again into the Drawing Room, where a profusion of Bride Cake was placed ready for refreshment; & salvers of rich wine, & a gold Cup containing an excellent mixture, were handed round. The Bride and Bridegrooms healths were drunk, & pieces of cake were drawn properly thro' the Wedding Ring for the dreaming Emolument of many spinsters and Batchelors.
>
> (Houblon 1907: 129–30)

An anonymous poem published in the London newspaper *St James's Chronicle* in 1799, contributed from nearby Surbiton, exploits the same, clearly well-known practice. The piece is written from the point of view of a bridesmaid and contains no suggestion that 'spinsters and Batchelors' alike would be dreaming.

> Enlivening source of hymeneal mirth,
> All hail the blest *Receipt* [i.e. recipe] that gave thee birth!
>
> Tho' Flora culls the fairest of her bowers,
> And strews the path of Hymen with her flowers;
> Not half the raptures give her scatter'd sweets,
> The *Cake* far kinder gratulation meets.
>
> The bride-maid's eyes with spark'ling glances beam,
> *She* views the *Cake* – and greets the *promis'd dream*.
> For when endow'd with necromantick spell,
> *She knows* what wond'rous things the *Cake* will tell.
>
> When from the altar comes the pensive bride,
> With down-cast looks – her partner by her side;

Soon from the ground these thoughtful looks arise,
To meet the *Cake* that gayer thought supplies.

With her own hand she charms each destined slice,
And thro' the ring repeats the *trebled thrice*.

The hallow'd ring infusing magick power,
Bids Hymen's visions wait the midnight hour:
The mystick treasure, plac'd beneath her head,
Will tell the fair – if haply she may wed.

A detailed account of similar but apparently more elaborate practices
from Lincolnshire appeared in *The Gentleman's Magazine* for 1832. This
time the restriction of the dreaming to the bride's friends, certainly girl
friends, is explicit. It may well be significant too that the groom now has
an active role prescribed.

> The just execution of this idolatrous ceremony is attended to with the
> most scrupulous exactness. The bride holds the ring between the
> fore-finger and the thumb of her right hand, through which the
> groom passes each portion of the cake nine times, previously cut by
> other individuals of the party into disposable pieces for the purpose.
> These he delivers in succession to the brides-maids, who seal them up
> carefully, each in an envelope of fair writing-paper. As amulets of
> inestimable value, they are distributed amongst the friends of the
> bride, who seldom neglect to make trial of their virtues. Various are
> the methods of augury to which they are applied, one only of which
> shall be mentioned here. If the fair idolatress deposit one of these
> amulets in the foot of her *left* stocking, when she goes to bed, and
> place it under her pillow, she will dream of the person who is destined
> by *fate* to be her partner for life.
>
> (Oliver 1832: 492)

A procedure for distribution has now appeared, and the directions for a
successful dreaming have been elaborated.

By this time the attitude of the educated classes to the practice had
clearly changed. From a topic for poems in Surbiton near London, it had
become ethnography to be reported from the countryside to an educated
and enquiring audience, and to be reported in a tone altogether different
to the simple acceptance displayed by the Rev. Abdy sixty years earlier.
In the countryside around Britain it survived a good deal longer
(Henderson 1866: 22–3; Henwood 1972: 68), but for the middle classes
it was on the way out. Identification of such practices with magic and
idolatry, even if they were not being taken wholly seriously, or a sexual

symbolism if that were even dimly perceived in pre-Freudian days, may have contributed to their disappearance in 'respectable' circles, but more likely to have been effective is its lack of fit with the wedding breakfast. This institution is discussed below as the basis for the next wave of ritual creation, in connection with cake-cutting. What appears to have been the last gasp in unpropitious surroundings of the earlier tradition was expressed in a *Manual for Ladies* (quoted in Laverack 1979: 116). Since, according to this source, a bride could not remove her wedding ring after the service, if cake were to be put through the ring it had to be done in advance. The task was assigned to the bridesmaids the day before the wedding. The pieces cut would then be 'wrapped up in ornamental papers of the latest novelty in design and colour and fastened with some pretty device [cf. Sherwood 1884: 71]. These mystic condiments are distributed at the wedding breakfast to the young unmarried guests with any desire to possess the "charming morsel".'[7] This compromise was not to last, but the dreaming continued. Cake on which to dream, though no longer put through the ring, was recorded in Swansea in the 1960s (Leonard 1980: 202) and in Glasgow, where special little white crêpe-paper bags in which to take the pieces home had commonly been provided, in the 1980s.

Other uses of the cake for divination in ways not focussed on the bride and therefore not confined to this particular kind of cake have also been recorded at times. In the nineteenth century, rings might be placed in both cakes and pies, particularly in Scotland and the north of England, with the idea that the finder of the ring would, like the fortunate catcher of the bride's bouquet in some places today – be the next married. Marchant offers instructions which, if followed, would have kept alive echoes of the dumb cake and offered an alternative use for cake-breaking suitable for the very different world of the late nineteenth century:

> Make a common flat cake of flour, water, currants, etc.; put therein a wedding ring and a sixpence.[8] When the company is about to retire on the wedding-day, the cake must be broken and distributed amongst the unmarried females. She who gets the ring in her portion of the cake will shortly be married; and the one who gets the sixpence will die an old maid.
>
> (Marchant 1879: 21)

A similar idea has been carried through the twentieth century by the 'charms' put into the Christmas pudding.

Jeaffreson and those who have followed him have wanted to integrate such varied 'cakes' and uses into a single account of the evolution of the wedding cake he knew later in the nineteenth century. Marchant, writing soon after Jeaffreson and wishing to follow him, suggests the way in which there may, as in Carr's northern Yorkshire and in many other marriage ceremonies, have been a cross-fertilisation of ideas. 'This practice', he writes,

> has now been modified by the bride cutting up and distributing the cake at the breakfast and amongst her friends; occasionally a plateful of cake, cut into small pieces, is thrown over the bride's head. The custom, however, of breaking a cake – but not *the* cake – over the bride's head on the threshold of the first house she enters still exists, we believe, in some parts of Scotland, the broken cake being made of oatmeal.
>
> (Marchant 1879: 90)

DISPLAY

Marchant, in distinguishing 'a cake' from '*the* cake', was in effect acknowledging the end of a lineage of bride cakes which had taken two or three centuries to disappear altogether. These cakes for breaking had had little in common, beyond the occasion of their use, with the wedding cake as it had been developed by the skills of bakers and confectioners over the same period. That was to last for at least a century more, and increasingly as the nineteenth century wore on, in the form of cakes for display. Display has indeed always been important but in the second half of the century it was beginning, at the top of society, to overwhelm their character as something to be eaten.

For the series of royal weddings discussed above, the official architectural and sculptural cakes were primarily display objects; it is not clear whether the cake within them, let alone their sugarpaste superstructures, was ever cut up and eaten (see p. 86 above). Certainly, separate cakes were provided not only for other occasions but for eating and for subsequent distribution too. On slightly less grand occasions, the problem of combining the two functions might also be solved by separate cakes. An instance from the great house of Mellerstain in the Borders is reported from about 1871 (Marshall 1983: 272–3). At a rather less exalted social level, a further solution is suggested by the catalogue (issued with Marchant 1879) of Messrs W. Hill, 'Caterers for Wedding Breakfasts, Cooks, Confectioners, Wine and Turtle Merchants, and Bakers to the Royal Family'. They were then offering not only 'Wedding Cakes, richly almond-iced and ornamented, decorated with Flowers, Sprays, Wreaths, &c.', priced from 21s. to £25, but also 'Plain

Almond-iced Wedding Cakes, For Cutting Up'. These were 2s. per lb, though they shared with their more spectacular fellows the essential quality: 'Every cake that Messrs. Hill and Co. send out has been kept until it has attained the highest possible condition of maturity.' Piping and tiering again made their contribution here. With their aid it became possible subsequently to produce impressive and elaborately decorated cakes which were nevertheless wholly destined to eating, if with the necessary aid of a saw, and often on successive occasions.

CUTTING THE CAKE

Even when the cakes discussed in preceding sections were of a form to require cutting, no particular significance attached to doing so. It seems to have been with the 'wedding breakfast', regarded in America as a specifically English innovation (Sherwood 1884: 68–9), that the cutting of the cake began to assume a significance of its own.

The breakfast became a distinctive meal, to be served after the wedding ceremony and before the departure of bride and groom. In form it consisted of an array of cold dishes set out on the table, savoury and sweet, with wine – particularly champagne – to drink. To this might be added courses served hot if required.[9]

A picture of such an event was published by Richard Doyle, a well-known caricaturist of early Victorian society, in 1850: see Figure 3. It was accompanied by a description in the form of an entry in 'Mr Pips hys Diary', contributed by Percival Leigh. The bride is described as being in white satin with orange flowers in her hair, the groom, 'a great Buck' in an incredible multi-coloured outfit. The men wore 'great White Favours at our Breasts, mighty conspicuous and, methought, absurd, the Things serving neither for Use nor Ornament'. The breakfast was 'very fine both for Show and Meats, every Dish ornamented with Flowers and Gimcracks, the cold Chickens trimmed with Ribbons, and the Bride-Cake, having upon it WAX CUPIDS and Turtle-Doves, was pretty'. Not one but two decorated cakes are actually shown in Doyle's picture, neither, it will be noticed, placed in front of the bride and groom. 'Mr Pips' describes the bridegroom as 'stiff and sheepish', the bride as 'shamefaced, and trying to hide her blushes with a Nosegay'.

He goes on, in what is by far the most informative account of such an event so far found:

> The Company first silent, till a Friend of the young Pair, who did say he had known them both from Babies, did propose their health in a pretty pathetic but confused Speech, and breaking down in the Midst

MANNERS· AND· CVSTOMS OF ᵞᵉ ENGLYSHE IN 1849   Nº 33.

┴A WEDDYNGE· ᴮREAKFASTE.

Figure 3 'A Weddynge Breakfaste', from Richard Doyle, *Manners and Customs of yᵉ Englyshe* (1850)

of a Sentence, conclude by wishing them long Life and Happiness, with great Applause. Then the Bride-Groom to return Thanks, but, perplexed with his Pronouns, obliged to stop short too, but, he said, overcome by his Feelings. The Champagne flowing, we soon merrier, especially an old Uncle of Dick's [the bridegroom] who began to make Jokes, which did trouble the Bride and Bride-Groom. But they presently with much Crying and Kissing and Shaking of Hands, away in a Coach-and-Four, amid the Cheering of the Crowd in the Street and the Boys shouting to behold the fine Equipage; and Servants and old Women looking on from the opposite Windows. We eating and drinking with great Delight till late in the Afternoon, but at last broke up, the Multitude saluting us each as we stepped into the Street, and the Policeman and Beadle that were guarding the Door in great State, touching their Hats. A grand Marriage Breakfast do give a brave

TABLEAU VIVANT.

Bridegroom (to his little Sister-in-Law at the Breakfast). "WELL, JULIE, YOU'VE GOT A NEW BROTHER NOW——"
Julie ("enfant terrible"). "YES; AND MA' SAID THE OTHER DAY TO PA', SHE DIDN'T THINK HE WAS MUCH ACCOUNT, ON'Y IT LOOKED LIKE LOTTIE'S LAST CHANCE!"
[Great clatter of Knives, Forks, and Spoons.

Figure 4 'Tableau Vivant': from *Punch* (1881)

Treat to the Mob, in Show, and to the Company in Eating and Drinking, and is great Fun to all but those most concerned.

(Doyle 1850: no pagination)

This is a picture of a celebration amongst 'Carriage-Company', amongst, that is to say, the upper classes to whom the wedding breakfast probably owes its origination. By this period in the middle of the century it had, however, probably become general amongst the middle classes too. Dickens in *Bleak House* (1853) has a marvellous account of the ill-assorted company at such an event in an impoverished middle-class setting.[10] There he mentions no cake, but an etiquette book published in London the following year, clearly referring to a gathering of much this kind, does assume a cake and shows clearly that something was, at this level of society if not amongst their betters, being made of the cutting.

> If the lady appears at breakfast, which is certainly desirable [but she may not be able to face the ordeal], she occupies, with her husband, the centre of the table, and sits by his side – her father and mother taking the top and bottom, and showing all honour to their guests. . . . The wedding-cake uniformly occupies the centre of the table. It is often tastefully surrounded with flowers, among which those of the fragrant orange ought to be conspicuous. After being cut according to the usages observed on such occasions . . . and everyone is helped – when, too, the health of the bride and bridegroom has been drunk, and every compliment and kind wish has been duly proffered and acknowledged, – the bride, attended by her friends, withdraws. . . .
>
> (Anon. 1854: 32–3)

Subsequently, the couple set off 'on their wedding journey'.

Exactly what 'the usages observed on such occasions' were in the middle of the century has not so far been documented, but by 1880 we can match a picture of an occasion (see Figure 4) to an explicit instruction. Here there is a cake on the table, though it is still unspectacular.

> It is the bride's duty to cut the cake. Of course an incision should previously be made. A knife is handed to her, which she puts in the cleft, and succeeds in getting a slice on to a plate. This is cut into small pieces, and handed round, and everybody is expected to partake.
>
> (Anon. 1880: 103)

It is the bride who is to cut the slice of cake which the company is then to share (Suzanne 1894: 232). This was an approach to the matter which was to last until the 1930s. M. & S. Bee, in their *Weddings without Worry*

(1935: 69), say: 'The bride should endeavour to cut out a good thick wedge, as this has to be broken up and handed round to the guests, all of whom must partake of it.'

By then, however, a new emphasis had been creeping in for some time. As wedding cakes became grander and more commonly tiered – there is no reference to tiers in these instructions – the cutting of the cake became more of a problem for more people. One solution was for a grand cake to have a pre-cut wedge in the base tier, iced lightly over.[11] From the 1930s or before, City Bakeries, a leading chain of bakers, confectioners and caterers in Glasgow, began to solve the bride's problem for her by cutting a wedge in this way. It was tied round with ribbon before being reinserted in the cake, and it could therefore be simply drawn out when needed. It became the distinguishing feature of the firm's cakes and as such it has since been retained, but it has been redundant for the greater part of its life. Mrs Beeton's 1923 edition of *The Book of Household Management* was already reflecting the movement of custom which was to make it so:

> The bride always cuts the first slice of cake, which is partaken of after the actual meal is finished. The cake is generally cut with a saw provided for the purpose, and as this is a rather hard task, the icing being somewhat difficult to cut through, it is generally considered sufficient if she makes the first incision.
>
> (Beeton 1923: 1392)

The accent, that is to say, was shifting away from the eating of cake which the bride had cut, onto the cutting itself. That it is the first slice and that she may be able to make only the first incision are new emphases. 'Mrs Beeton' continued to give her readers this same instruction until 1950.

A more striking shift had begun long before this, however. Already in the 1930s the task was beginning to be redefined as a joint one. Another wedding book, Carol Inman's *ABC of Weddings* (1938), has the groom assisting the bride in the difficult task. A picture of Joe Loss, a well-known band leader, posed with his left hand over his new wife's right, has him 'assisting' her in this way at their wedding in the same year (*Good Housekeeping* 1989: 87). This was a formula which 'Mrs Beeton' eventually adopted and was still promulgating in 1980.

By this route the joint 'cutting of the cake' as a procedure remote from the practical business of cutting up pieces for serving to guests was created.[12] It was to become one of the clearest and most essential rites of marrying in the remainder of the twentieth century. In the 1980s the procedure was detailed thus:

The bride holds the knife in her right hand, with the bridegroom's right hand on hers, and her left hand on top. After the first slice has been successfully dealt with, the cake can be taken away and cut into small pieces for the guests to eat with their coffee.

(Derraugh 1983: 55)

It was also one of the most potentially meaningful. An encyclopedia new in the 1980s noted, of an English buffet-style wedding reception: 'Its centrepiece, the lucky white-iced wedding cake, should be cut by bride and groom together, as their first joint task in life' (Kightly 1986: 230).

This is not, as we already know, the end of the story. The joint cutting, already removed from the effective cutting up, is used again as the subject of one of the series of essential 'official' wedding photographs. In this form it is a further stage removed from the practical cutting up. Now the knife is merely poised, as if ready for the insertion. The Japanese development may here be recalled from Chapter 2. The 'cake' when it appears in Japan, having ceased to be edible or to be cut up, a mere poising of the knife has no cutting to refer to. The knife is therefore plunged in, a slot and the mechanism already described being provided for the purpose. As a ceremony this is left in danger of complete separation from the chain of actions from which historically it derived. It becomes the occasion of a dramatic photograph and may perhaps, as a joint but eventually incomprehensible task for bride and groom, become a suitable marker for the liminal state of bridal togetherness, before the detachment of marriage is finally established (Lebra 1984: 124 ff.)

KEEPING IT FOR THE CHRISTENING

The 1980s wedding book already quoted notes that 'You may wish to reserve the top tier to keep for a christening' (Derraugh 1983: 55). This was a suitably permissive way of putting it for an avowedly up-to-date book. It was an age in which many of those marrying could be expected to be so deep in debt to pay for the house they would be buying that any thought of babies would need to be set aside. But what had in fact become established was the idea that the top should be kept, not for *a* christening but for *the* christening. The cake in this way incorporated the idea of a baby to be born into the very event of the wedding itself. It persisted in doing so into a period when reproduction and marriage were being increasingly delinked (cf. Leonard 1980: 203).

Long before there was any question of multi-tier wedding cakes, christenings had been amongst the special occasions for which cakes might be made. Pepys joined in the celebration of a christening with a cake in London on 17 July 1664 and Aubrey (1881: 65, 139), late in that century, noted that 'We still use Cakes at Christnings [sic]'.

Such cakes then pass unnoticed until the nineteenth century. Henderson's first edition of 1793 has only bride cakes, but the new edition prepared by Schnebellie in 1805 substitutes a recipe for a wedding or christening cake 'made exactly the same as at Tupp and Perry's in Oxford Street' [where Schnebellie had been apprenticed, in London] (Henderson 1805: 213–14). This set the pattern. Mrs Beeton also bracketed rich bride and christening cake with a single recipe in her first edition of 1861. As the wedding cake grew grander, however, though the christening cake remained similar in being iced and decorated in white and in the same formal style, it became an increasingly unequal running mate (Davies 1892: 8–9). Into the twentieth century it would still sometimes be assumed to require the same high quality of ingredients as the wedding cake, but, as Vine noted from a commercial point of view 'somehow, as the christenings come at intervals and the birthdays get more numerous, the quality of the cake has to be reduced to increase its size as the circle gets larger who have to partake of it' (n.d.: 215).

It was probably well into the twentieth century before, at some unremarked moment, the idea that the first christening could be provided for from the wedding cake itself was born. An etiquette book of 1902 which describes the uses of the cake in detail makes no mention of the possibility: at that time cake beyond what was needed for the reception was required for sending out in boxes to special friends, for pieces to give to the guests to take home with them, and for the bride's first 'At Home' days when she had settled into her own house (Anon. 1902: 76–7).[13] Once, however, the idea of using it for the christening had appeared, instructions for keeping the top tier in good condition began to be issued and confectioners would offer to re-ice their cakes free for this purpose. When three tiers became the norm, to be bought regardless of the amount of cake needed for the wedding itself, there were sure often to be tops left after the day. A christening provided at least a sufficiently important and even relevant occasion for disposing of them. It might then seem to people looking for an explanation of the three tiers that there would have to be one for the reception, one for distribution and one for the christening.

When no christening was anticipated, alternative uses would be found, for house-warming, birthdays, Christmas or even the first birthday of a child already born. Though no regular pattern had been established, two other contrasting possibilities were encountered in the

Glasgow research. A cake might, perhaps most often, be made part of a first anniversary. This was not new (Leonard 1980: 203) but was in effect following established American practice. The emphasis would be on the couple themselves and their relationship, and even implicitly perhaps on their achievement in being still together a year later. The time scale needed to be short for styles of cake which only the freezer would preserve for as long as a year. With very different implications, cakes were found in the Glasgow research being used in the silver-wedding celebrations of parents (Charsley 1991: 40). They were then making a link between the weddings of succeeding generations, expressing through the cake a sense of continuity. Now, however, it was not the new generation to be christened with whom the link was to be made, but the old.

CONCLUSION: USES AND FORMS

> Of course there are quieter weddings and very simple arrangements as to serving refreshments: a wedding-cake and a decanter of sherry often are alone offered to the witnesses of a wedding.

Mrs Sherwood wrote this in her Anglo-American etiquette of 1884, and much the same thing could have been said on either side of the Atlantic throughout the succeeding century. However simple the celebration of a wedding, it was highly unusual for there not to be a cake to be shared with those present.

It might also, as we have noted, be sent through the post to others who were not present, or even be given a recognised place in the new wife's first entertaining. The same etiquette book quoted above notes that it was formerly part of the bridesmaids' duty to go to the bride's (parents') home on the day following the wedding to cut up, box and address pieces of the bride cake. But

> of recent years, no doubt with a view to economising time, and to restore order speedily in the upturned household, a list is given to the firm that provided the cake, and they take the responsibility for sending it out. The usual charge for doing so is about 12s. per dozen boxes, with an extra 2d. for postage. The pieces of cake at this price will weigh about a quarter of a pound.
>
> (Anon. 1902: 62)

This smacks of advertising. In later years, far smaller pieces were the norm and few would expect – or perhaps even regard it as proper – to have the job done commercially for them.

What this chapter has shown is that having a cake is only a starting point. Once there is one and it has acquired a primary association with the wedding, there are a range of other ways in which it can be exploited. Such uses may remain secondary, in merely utilising given potentials: the use of the cake for cutting has affected its form only very marginally, in the addition of glycerine to some icing mixtures and in the pre-cutting which some firms perform for the benefit of their fellows in the trade who will have in reality to cut the cake up. It was, on the contrary and as has been seen, the difficulty of cutting which conditioned the evolution of this particular use. Using a part of the cake for the christening likewise exploits the keeping qualities of the cake without affecting its form in any way. Display is, however, different. It becomes a primary use of the cake and the basis on which the trade could develop ever more lavish and costly possibilities. It is more difficult to be certain of the negative case, but cake-breaking seems to have altered in part because it was incompatible with the kind of thing the wedding cake had become, as well as because it was incompatible with what the bride was becoming. Use may therefore affect form where very basic human motivations are involved, but more commonly it is in the opposite direction that causation works here: forms suggest possibilities for use.

9 Meanings and interpretation

Preceding chapters have examined the evolving forms of cakes and the uses which have been made of them. These chapters have necessarily involved us with meaning in all its basic senses. We have seen how English terms, 'cake' and 'icing' in particular, acquired their contemporary meanings as the objects to which they refer evolved. We have seen how bride cakes and wedding cakes changed from being cakes which happened to have been baked for weddings to highly distinctive structures, instantly announcing their association with a wedding. As such they indicate weddings, as in Dickens's *Cricket on the Hearth* (1846/1971: 34): ' "it's my belief that if you was to pack a wedding-cake up in a tea-chest, or a turn-up beadstead, or a pickled salmon keg, or any unlikely thing, a woman would be sure to find it out directly." ' And they can be used as markers for weddings and even marriage (cf. Goode *et al.* 1984: 207).[1] We have seen indeed that they have come to do this not only within their own societies of origin but, as a widely meaningful element of 'western culture', in many other countries across the world. In examining uses, we saw dimensions of meaning necessarily being added for those familiar with them. This was most spectacularly illustrated by the bridesmaid's poem of 1799, quoted in full in the preceding chapter:

> The bride-maid's eyes with spark'ling glances beam,
> *She* views the *Cake* – and greets the *promis'd dream*.

The cake for the young lady envisaged here, and doubtless for generations of young participants in weddings, meant not just the part it played in the event itself but 'the promis'd dream' too.

These are all meanings which are real and important. They are the basics at which historians and anthropologists elucidating unfamiliar cultures always need to work (Charsley 1987a: 101 ff.) Frequently, however, people have the idea that there are or may be in their own and others' practices further kinds of meaning which a student of the society has to regard as optional extras. In principle there could be ideas which everybody 'knows' and to which everybody subscribes. There are, for instance, meanings in Catholic ritual, in particular the meaning of the bread and wine in the mass, which are taught as a qualification for participation and, as far as this central rite is concerned, constantly reiterated in the ritual text itself. There may also be esoteric meanings which, though 'known' only to a few, have a special claim to being 'real' since those who possess them control the system. The use of access to such 'secret' knowledge as a resource for control occurs only in nooks and crannies in contemporary western societies but is much more familiar to anthropologists of Melanesia and other regions of the world (e.g. Barth 1977: 217 ff.; La Fontaine 1977; Keesing 1982: 38–9). Popular ritual, however, if it is not part of any organised institution, is bound to be provided much less systematically with extra meanings.

From the point at which the cake emerged as a focus of research for the present author, it was clear that few people in recent years had been thinking about it other than as an essential expense associated with a wedding. It did not emerge in typical anthropological fashion, that is to say, as something the importance of which was taught to the anthropologist by those whose lives were being studied. As recounted elsewhere (Charsley 1987a: 105–6), it was the symbolic imagination of the anthropologist looking for pattern and meaning which found a problem here. The initial field research did not therefore set out to look for extra meanings. Though it was always ready to pick up any that were offered, conspicuously here they were not.

Subsequently, explicit requests for meanings, posed particularly to makers of wedding cakes, confirmed that the ideas available were few, little developed, and not of any wide concern. This later research included a postal enquiry of a small sample of cake-manufacturers around Britain, results from which have already been used in earlier chapters.[2] These correspondents were asked why they thought cakes were so important for weddings and what meaning they saw in the cutting of the cake. The two questions were not intended to tap different kinds of information but to give two chances to elicit whatever ideas might be available. In the event, out of the sixteen who replied, three omitted to answer either question and four more offered something for one or the other only. Though there may have been exceptions, the pattern here suggested an inability to think of a satisfactory answer rather than an unwillingness to embark on what might have been a tricky topic.

Of those who did respond to the first part, 'tradition' was the answer of four, as of others encountered in the earlier study. It is possible that they were thinking of the cake as maintaining a practice valued for the connection it makes with the past. One other correspondent wrote: 'throughout the ages a confection of some kind has been a symbol of fertility and abundance' and saw the modern cake as the heir to this tradition. She took up, that is to say, the theme the Victorian writers developed and which was discussed above as 'the Victorian myth of origin', but she was unusual in doing so. I have myself tried to put into circulation a richer and more historically reliable version of traditional meaning.[3] In summary:

> The wedding cake, in its mixture, its marzipan and its icing, therefore represents a rich celebratory past in which the glories of the Victorian age are strongly featured. Its display and tasting might represent a significant participation in a long tradition of English feasting – if only the participants were aware of it.
>
> (Charsley 1987b: 14)

It is, however, unlikely that anything so elaborate was intended by those who simply wrote 'tradition'. In discussion, they might well have echoed the manager of a leading wedding-cake firm quoted in the first chapter. He, it will be recalled, distinguished between tradition and convention. It was, he thought, really only the latter: because others have cakes, you do too.

The only other answer to which several correspondents subscribed was the idea which we saw as the culmination of the evolution of cake-cutting, the idea that it is a first joint action on the part of the newly-weds. This represents an elementary but interesting kind of interpretation which merely highlights a possible description of the action concerned. As an account of what is happening it can scarcely be denied; what is disputable and therefore interesting is the salience attached to it. Four referred to it; nine who mentioned other things did not. To the limited extent that there is any standard contemporary meaning, this has to be it.

Other meanings offered were marginally more complex, sliding from description to metaphor and introducing hints of the symbolic. The couple were described as 'sharing the richness with friends and family'. This is of course to highlight a distinct aspect of the use of the cake, its distri-bution, but it is more complex in calling on an acknowledged attribute of the cake, richness, and suggesting – so inexplicitly that again it can hardly be challenged – a symbolic dimension to the sharing. A recent writer on customs and culture of food offers a similar embedded and inexplicit symbolism here: 'The wedding cake is traditionally shared out amongst guests so that blessings and happiness can be shared' (Fieldhouse 1986: 98).

The correspondent above, and one other in the survey who suggested that the couple were, in cutting the cake, at 'the beginning of a fruitful life together', were the only ones in the whole research experience to make anything, even as slight as this, of the composition of the cake itself. Victorian writers might, however, espouse the theme of richness and make more of it than any modern. Queen Victoria's wedding cake was described as 'consisting of all the most exquisite compounds of all rich things with which the most expensive cakes can be composed, mingled and mixed together with delightful harmony by the most elaborate science of the confectioner' (Hindley 1878: 354). Marchant (1879: 81) enthused about such cakes in general: 'The pure white covering, symbolical of the virgin purity of the bride; the multifarious ingredients blended with such skill that everyone tastes, though none predominates, the intermixture being typical of the union of the two lives; the lusty orange yields its candied peel;' and more in the same vein.

Since our set does not include any explicitly symbolic interpretation, we shall return to the further possibilities of this below. What it does include is three examples which invoke the principle used so memorably by Van Gennep (1909) for his classic theory of rites of passage (see Chapter 8, note 6 above). This is the principle which asserts that customary actions are to be understood as performed metaphors which are effective in bringing about the situation they represent. Cutting the cake, wrote one correspondent, was the couple 'taking the plunge' into their new life. Here an almost dead linguistic metaphor for beginning something is resurrected by framing it in quotation marks. It is then used to make a link to the action of 'plunging' the knife into the cake, suggesting thereby that this is an effective metaphorical performance. A second suggestion of the same general type went a little beyond merely describing the action of cutting as joint – considered above – and suggested that it bound the couple together. Here the reasoning is less clear and in terms of the more obvious metaphors to which Van Gennep usually draws attention it is paradoxical, the cut that binds.[4] The third example did however call on this obvious link though for a less obvious purpose. It suggested that the cutting severed the bride and groom's links with the past and prepared for their future together. Outside the survey and moving away from cutting, a catering manageress in the earlier study called on the idea of reciprocity to ground her version of the effective, acted metaphor. She considered that the giving of favours by the bride was a repaying of her debt to all those who had helped her to get married. She would then be able to start married life with no debts, free of emotional ties, with only her husband to concentrate on. Few, she added, had any idea of why they were giving favours away, as few perhaps as have any idea of severing ties in cutting their cake.

There are, therefore, various possible ideas about extra meanings of an effective nature in the customary actions surrounding the cake. A well-known writer on baking and confectionery brings in the ideas of ritual and function to make a more difficult link, between the actions of some and effects for others. He sees the eating of small pieces of the cake by guests and others as 'a ritual to help seal a marriage and to wish God-speed to the happy couple in their new life' (Littlewood 1989 (Part 7): 28).[5] 'Wishing God-speed' is something that the eaters themselves can be taken as doing – though it would certainly be a surprise to many – whereas 'sealing a marriage', though it has the same useful ambiguity of metaphor, they presumably cannot effect on their own: their action may therefore help.

This is therefore to enlarge the range of meanings attached to cakes by the makers of them who responded to the survey. Those meanings have indeed now been exhausted. There are however two sources of a more adventurous type of symbolic interpretation. One is the account of their own experience offered by a couple within the original Glasgow study and already set out in the first chapter above; the other is the anthropologist's own symbolic imagination, let loose at the same period of the research though separately, on the practices, present and past, which were being discovered (cf. Edwards 1982).

It will be recalled that the account obtained from the couple derived from two separate interviews, one with the groom before the wedding, the other with the bride after it. The first was conducted by my research assistant, the second by myself. Neither was altogether easy. In the first the groom explained their decision not to have a cake by noting that 'someone said' that the cutting symbolised the bride 'surrendering her virginity'. When subsequently the issue was taken up with the bride, it turned out that she was convinced that 'everything to do with weddings has its symbols and meanings'. Previously, she thought, people knew that the cutting of the cake meant the bride losing her virginity: 'the way the groom puts his hand on the bride's, so it's not just her; it's him too. A horrible idea!' She felt also that the bride wearing a white dress would be announcing her virginity, unfair since the groom's outfit said nothing about himself. 'Very sexist!' as the groom had commented. Such ideas were, as has been stressed, highly unusual in the research experience. Though a need to fend off possible implications of not wearing white by explaining their motivation was sometimes felt, few saw the standard white dress as proclaiming anything beyond their role as bride (Charsley 1991: 66–73). As for the whiteness of the cake, the Victorian preoccupation with whiteness and purity, exemplified in the quotation from Marchant above, had receded without being entirely forgotten: the manager cited above referred to 'the virginal white' of most of the cakes he was still sending out. This couple's preoccupation was therefore unusual but in no way idiosyncratic.

The symbolic possibilities here were not at the time elaborated. The anthropological imagination, the second source, seized on the same idea but developed it, perhaps characteristically, to explain a wide range of practice. It started not with the cutting of the cake but with its form. The characteristic shape and colour of the bride, veiled and in full white dress, appeared to be echoed in the shape and colour of the cake. The cake could therefore stand for the bride. A richly minable symbolic vein was immediately opened up and it turned out to be one which seems, like Van Gennep's scheme on a far more general level, to reveal a coherence in what is done which would not otherwise be apparent.

If cake and white-dressed bride are in some sense one and the same, it is not surprising that these are the two objects which identify and represent 'the wedding' most inevitably. If the bride is wearing near-white – cream, champagne, ivory or whatever – it has been noted that the cake is commonly expected to match. Favours in Scotland appear in a new and more meaningful light. We have seen in Chapter 7 above that they were once lightly attached to the bride's clothes. This was before the advent of the white-dress-and-cake pattern. The bride's favours had therefore found their way from her person to the cake, from which they could be more decorously taken off and distributed. If the cake represents the bride herself, the close identification between her and what might otherwise be regarded – and indeed in England are usually regarded – as no more than cake decorations again becomes part of a powerful if normally unseen pattern. The bride carries a bouquet, the cake its favours, often in the form of artificial flowers; it was noticeable that amongst our informants there was resistance to the idea of tossing bouquets, to be caught by the next bride, though this was well known to happen elsewhere. The bouquet, as indeed all the flowers around, is commonly treated as if it were itself the prime favour.

It is the cutting, however, which is given the most striking new significance if the cake is identified with the bride. Plunging the knife into the centre of the cake breaks through the 'virginal white' outer shell. It is something the couple do together. The pre-cutting of cakes by manufacturers has already been discussed. It is only on inner layers though; there is still a shell to be broken through. This operation is called, somewhat anomalously as has already been seen, 'cutting the cake', but significance can now be seen in the fact that it is a matter of plunging the knife in rather than producing slices for serving. It might even be suggested that the name is a diversionary euphemism. Finally, there is the matter of the top tier, set aside for the christening. As the salience of contraception in modern life makes us now well aware, procreation is not the same thing as sexual inauguration, but a linking of the two in the context of the wedding, if this is indeed what is happening, would scarcely be surprising.

The potential for symbolic interpretation here is striking therefore. What is argued, however, is that such interpretation, far from representing the discovery of some underlying reality, is the way human imagination may play amongst the plethora of materials for interpretation thrown up by the patterns of repetitive action found in all societies. It plays only occasionally and highly selectively, except amongst certain anthropologists and liturgists (Charsley 1991: 195–9 and *passim*). Often its playing makes no difference to the evolution of practice – this is discussed more generally in the next and final chapter – but occasionally it does. It does because people invent or modify practices to conform to symbolic ideas. The interplay between whiteness, understood explicitly as representing purity, and cake-decoration in the nineteenth century is a clear instance of a positive relationship. It is a negative which provides the most striking link identified in this research however. The couple who identified the cutting as sexual symbolism did not have a cake. Practice is vulnerable, this suggests, to interpretation attaching unacceptable meanings to it.

This must be so, but the case considered carefully leads to a slightly different conclusion. In the first place, as an idea, this symbolic link has been available since joint cutting evolved in the first half of the twentieth century. It has to be imagined that the thought will have crossed many minds in that period. It has indeed been printed at least twice. None of this has so far had any impact on the popularity of the cake. Why then did it affect this particular couple? Not, it is clear, because the meaning in itself blocked the cake but because of the way this couple attached the meaning to further interests which were important to them in the context of their marriage. The effect of the supposed sexual significance was amplified, that is to say, by being linked, through the idea of the bride making declarations about herself which were not required of the groom, to feminist concerns with equality. The lesson to be drawn from the case is not therefore that symbolic interpretation can in any way readily undermine practice. Few would take symbolic meaning in itself that seriously. But linked into wider and more practical concerns it may occasionally do so.

10 Towards a theory of cultural change?

Underlying the charting of change in preceding chapters has been a concern with its principles. We have been examining not merely a story of happenings but the nature and processes of cultural change, as exemplified in a field where it is unusually well documented. An idea of the nature and processes of such change has underpinned the work, hardly a theory, merely a way of conceptualising change, and in some ways a negative one at that. It is a conception which distrusts such grand ideas as 'culture', 'society' and 'structure', and their less fashionable fellows 'custom' and 'tradition'. It sees them as ideas which are often useful servants in the struggle to express meaning but are as beguiling as they are misleading when reified. When custom appears to be king, society to have its demands, or structure is thought to constitute some kind of underlying reality, tools of thought have escaped their proper domain; thinking has gone badly wrong (cf. Barth 1989).

The actors in cultural change cannot therefore be any of these things, neither custom, nor society, nor structure; they can only be individual people each with their own experience. Cultural change means people coming to act differently and to regard the new ways as normal and even proper. To that extent they are necessarily thinking and valuing differently too, though consciousness of change may be less or more or indeed quite other than the historian, who is able to review evidence drawn from the past, assesses it. Change occurs as people bring their sense of what should be done, grounded in past experience, to the test of action in the present. What occurs, influenced by any or all the varied factors which impinge on people's lives, sometimes challenges expectations derived from the past. It will then add a new component to the experience of those involved and the possibility of changed expectations for the future. Such is the very general conception, almost an anti-theory, on which the present enterprise has been grounded.

It is certainly less than a theory in that it offers no hope of deductively predicting what will in any given case happen. What this study has contributed to building up – and what I think is all that can be done in the study of people and the way they conduct their lives – is a grounded sense of the way things typically work out, a phenomenology of cultural change. The great contribution of anthropology to human knowledge has been the construction of phenomenologies of social forms and cultural possibilities. With the phenomenology of cultural change we have so far been less conspicuously successful. The final task here will therefore be to set out the phenomena which have been identified.

OBJECTS, CUSTOM AND MEANINGS

Something more has however to be said about the kinds of evidence which have been examined here. The study has focussed on objects but objects which are, more directly and completely than most, materialised customary action. Cakes, like other complex foods, are the product of the specialised form of custom called recipes. They last for a relatively short time beyond the actions which produce them, and in this time they are made part of other sequences of customary action which are predicated upon them. In the process meanings of various kinds are associated with them, occasionally meanings of the esoteric kind which require interpretation for their revelation. It is unnecessary here therefore to draw any firm line between objects and practices. The wedding cake and the wedding breakfast or reception are both the products of following instructions. Both evolve in basically the same way, with each cake and each event potentially contributing to the experience of those involved with them, and each pattern established constituting the reality from which people may in some way move on.

Objects and their recipes do nevertheless have a certain autonomy and relative simplicity. Though the instructions may be complex and the skills required considerable, technical constraints are such that, if the object is to be produced at all, the ways in which individual specimens can vary from one another are limited when compared with the possible variations between individual customary performances. The wedding cake may be useful as a marker for weddings just because it is relatively invariant. Even such objects are to a degree distinctive therefore. They enter the field of cultural change as a kind of sheet-anchor. They do not, that is to say, immobilise but they slow drift. They also constitute a point at which individuals, by as it were raising the anchor or changing its design, may contribute to future patterns with a kind of directness and occasional visibility which is rare otherwise. We do not know for certain that Mrs Raffald invented the double icing but it makes sense to think that she did, just as Trevor-Roper (1983) can propose an inventor for the Scottish kilt. What is certain is that this one person, Elizabeth Raffald of Manchester, by taking up and promulgating the double-icing scheme, was instrumental in changing custom.

Objects suggest too a conception of the way in which innovations are taken up. Mrs Raffald's book through all its numerous editions secured publicity for her scheme. It proposed it to thousands of readers, the majority of whom doubtless either did not notice it, were not thinking of making a bride cake, did not have the required facilities, did not feel confident enough to tackle it, had their own valued way of making such a cake, or were simply not interested. We have direct evidence however that some did take it up. Through a process of cumulative individual choice, no doubt involving repeated pioneering in particular circles and the influence of example, it gradually became, over the period of a century, the established norm. In the case of piping, we know that it was not invented by those who, in the 1890s, took it up and vigorously publicised it, but their initiative in promoting it not just as an addition to the cake-decorator's resources but as an alternative form of decoration was what made the difference. In a more rapidly changing world and chiefly through the more quickly responsive network of commercial producers by then established, we know that this revolution was accomplished much more quickly, something like a decade rather than a century. The trade at this period was well adjusted to testing innovations on the market; it was what people would buy more than what home-bakers would choose to make which was controlling the evolution of the cake.

The conception of cultural change suggested here is thus in a general and unsophisticated sense a market model. Innovations are proposed, at base by each individual performance which departs from expectations, intentionally or even by accident. An innovation which gets no more publicity than amongst those who directly experience it is unlikely to go further, simply because few who might be interested in it, might approve of it and have either the opportunity or the necessary resources to take it up will ever know about it. There is always a small chance that it will, however. Publicity changes the situation, though not fundamentally as long as the individual adoption of new or modified practices is necessary. From the mid-nineteenth century there was publicity for the wedding cakes and practices of royalty, and etiquette writers began, hesitantly as we have seen, to offer instruction on wedding practices. This is the Raffald model: many may know but few choose; change occurs only gradually and cumulatively. Publicity in itself speeds the possible and likely rate of change but does not change the way it has to occur. The 1890s model of commercial innovation marks a more fundamental shift. Only gradually, but conspicuously by the 1980s, has there developed what can properly be called a wedding industry. This has moved into a direct commercialisation of popular rites, controlling and marketing them as a product like any other (Charsley 1991). Altogether more dramatic rates of change become possible.

How then do objects, uses and meanings interact? There can be little doubt that this history shows the established object as likely to condition use and meaning rather than vice versa, and that object and use normally condition meaning. Sadly perhaps, the anthropologist has to conclude that the kinds of meaning in which practitioners of the subject have often specialised are usually extraneous to cultural development. Objects come first, their uses follow, and human imagination playing around both occasionally proposes meanings.

There are however exceptions. Amongst uses, display has at times influenced the evolution of the cake. That it should be the grandest possible has been important, but only when it was combined, as it was in the late nineteenth and early twentieth centuries – and possibly again in the late twentieth – with an eye to commercial advantage. Apart from this there have been only a few hints and marginal influences to be observed. In the Victorian period the 'new form' of wedding cake, with alternating layers of marzipan and cake, may have been intended better to satisfy those to whom pieces to eat would be distributed. It survived hardly long enough to be recorded for posterity. Later, the idea that a square cake would cut up better has often been mentioned and perhaps had some impact on promoting the shape, but if so it was not a powerful enough factor to prevent its retreat in the most recent period. Pre-cutting under the icing is more certain but very marginal to the form of the cake.

Form has on the other hand always conditioned use. Cake-breaking did not keep breakable cakes in demand for weddings; its end was associated with the spread of the plum cake. The keeping quality of the cake allowed pieces of it to be distributed after the wedding and the top tier to be associated with the christening. The difficulty of cutting a grand royal-iced cake was the basis for the evolution of the joint cutting. Was it perhaps the plainness of Scottish styles of cake decoration which allowed cakes there to become vehicles for favours? But it does not seem likely that this use is going to hold back the adoption of the new sugarpaste style which does not offer scope for it. Rather, the practice will adapt to the form.

For meanings the exceptions are even harder to find. It seems likely that items may occasionally have been included in the mixture for wedding cakes out of a sense of their symbolic appropriateness, though explicit evidence of this is scarce. A small amount of bitter almond has sometimes been added to sweet almonds (e.g. Jack 1907: 98),[1] and it has been suggested that this may have been intended to symbolise the measure of pain to be expected amongst the pleasures of marriage. The fact that marzipan might at one time be called 'love' may similarly have been a reason for its inclusion within the 'new form' cake mentioned above. But this is falling back on speculation. The clearest case of effective meaning is the way the association of whiteness with purity held the Victorian cake, at some periods rigorously, to the colour – or lack of it – which it had inherited, even determining the kinds of flower which would be used for its decoration. Such things are possible therefore, though uncommon. It is, as has been seen, even possible for attributions of meaning to make its standard use, cutting, impossible and hence to prevent people having a cake altogether, though the circumstances for this were, we noted, necessarily special.

PHENOMENA OF CULTURAL CHANGE

Objects as determinants

Though there are therefore exceptions, objects tend to condition their uses, and objects and uses together to condition the meanings that may be attached to them. If this is so of objects so close to action as we have been examining, it is likely to be even more so of those which are less dependent for their creation on human action or which, once each individual specimen has been created, stay around as permanent assets, resources or constraints. Uses may however evolve independent of any change in the object. The array of outcomes of such evolution was noted for cake-breaking, though none of the ways in which any of them actually occurred can be documented. For cake-cutting, evolving in the twentieth century against the background of an unchanging cake, more in the way of documentation has been available. For the factors which may influence such evolution we have to look to others of our phenomena below. It means, however, that technological change will always have an impact on customary practices but that it is by no means the only source of change in them.

Marooning

One of the less obvious ways in which technological change produces cultural change which is highlighted in the history of the wedding cake I have termed 'marooning'. It is a phenomenon to which Cannadine alludes in his study of the British monarchy: what is common, even standard and merely practical, at one time, assumes a new aspect when it is prolonged into an era of changed practices and practicalities. Cannadine (1983: 145–6) notes the way in which royal ritual, invigorated in an age of European competition, became an apparently British speciality when other royalty had largely disappeared. At a more detailed level, he notes how the mode of ceremonial travel became special by virtue of retaining horse-drawn carriages when all around they were being replaced with cars. Of the 1930s he writes: 'by now the monarch's mode of conveyance, already unusual and grand in the preceding period, had become positively fairytale' (Cannadine 1983: 123–4, 142–3).

For the wedding cake, it was the way it retained, in Britain but not in the United States, the spiced, rich-fruit mixture which had been the form in which cake first developed. As other forms were developed and other ideas imported, cakes for weddings were left behind and became thereby distinctive in a way that they had not been before. More spectacularly, the cake's white icing, at first standing only for quality, became a characteristic of a cake for wedding use when coloured icings began to be used freely on other cakes. Marooning is not of course the only possibility: we saw too the attempt of confectioners in Edinburgh to do something different, to differentiate wedding cakes as pink, but it was marooning in England which won out over innovation in Scotland. As far as the style of decoration is concerned, here again it was initially the marooning of the wedding cake as a plain white-iced cake as decoration for Twelfth and other cakes developed. Its plainness acquired an altogether new significance, before new and quite different styles of decoration, culminating in piping, were developed for it.

These examples have all been towards the object end of the object-practice continuum. They have resulted in distinctive forms which might provoke speculation about meanings and assumptions about purposes, both of which would be historically unjustified. On the other side, for what are clearly practices, the effects can be more dramatic, though there is no more than a hint of it in our history. When bread, let alone cake, ceases to be broken or even breakable, then any example of such breaking which persists is marooned. It is deprived of much of its context, becomes to a degree mysterious and open to interpretation. If it is not done with any clear practical intent it is ready to provoke the conclusion that it must be expressive in nature. The part played by marooning in generating some of the more surprising 'rituals' of humanity deserves to be considered.

Tradition

Why does marooning occur? Is it not an attachment to tradition which produces it? If so it is oddly selective, since it is a phenomenon produced by change. In fact it is clear that a variety of circumstances can produce the effect. It may be sheer accident: there is no connection between the persistence of British royal ritual and the disappearance of other monarchies. It may be a technical matter: we saw how the wedding cake was left initially as large but flat when other foods were rising high. This was because it was already too large to be made to rise by the means being applied at the time to other foods. Cannadine does not, unfortunately, relate exactly why the older form of transport was retained for royal ceremonial use: available alternatives may at first have been thought insufficiently reliable, or not to offer appropriate facilities, or there may have been some other reason such as their country of manufacture which made them unsuitable. The dates of key events in relation to technological advance may even have been important here. But it is likely too that 'tradition' did have its part to play.

Whereas regular events happening frequently may simply follow an established pattern, events which happen only infrequently, and especially if each is regarded as of great moment, are perforce different. How they can and should be performed necessarily becomes a question and it is almost inevitable that past occasions will be considered. Where the past is positively valued and precedent is clear it may seem important to people to follow it. This certainly occurred in the exceptional circumstances of the Second World War. As early as 1940 the use of sugar for the external decoration of cakes was prohibited (Bennion & Stewart 1945: 247). Far from this and the growing shortages which followed precipitating any new form of wedding cake, there was a conscious struggle to preserve as much of established tradition as was possible. Paper decorations might be stuck on cakes with gum, and cardboard wedding-cake shells appeared, some even with tiers. Any small and inevitably more or less inappropriate cake which could be procured for the celebration might be covered with such a shell. Having a proper wedding cake was identified as tradition, despite the lack of almost all the ingredients which had been required for such a cake (Longmate 1971: 158–60). This was a short-run development, assumed always to be a temporary expedient and having, as far as has been discovered, no effect on practice in the longer run. Where adequate precedent is not immediately available, a creative reworking of whatever record there may be is possible, as with Jeaffreson's myth of the origins of the wedding cake (see Chapter 3 and *passim*; Samuel & Thompson 1990: 20).

But even if the past is not given any special value, there is only one other option for events of importance. That is to find something new and special, to exceed the past. A potlatch effect is very familiar to anthropologists in exchange institutions around the world. Particularly in periods of expanding resources and technological advance, but even at other times (Llewellyn-Davies 1984), there are striking instances of the way in which periodic rituals may be made special by new additions (e.g. Nairn & Strathern 1974). Both the new and tradition may of course be called on in the same event.

Something more like a principle of cultural change lies behind the phenomenon of marooning therefore. Tradition and precedent are implicated but not, I am suggesting, in quite the manner in which they have been thought to bind certain societies but not our own. There is no cause to distinguish, as does Hobsbawm (1983a: 2), between custom and invented tradition. Invention may always have a part to play in the origination and modification of custom in all societies, and in no society does invention become tradition without being taken up and becoming part of the taken-for-granted apparatus in terms of which people conduct their lives. The idea of 'the invention of tradition' is, however, usefully drawing attention to a variability in cultural creativeness and its peculiar vigour in many areas of life in the decades around the turn of the twentieth century. This essay has sought to throw a little light on one small corner of this major phenomenon.

As far as marooning is concerned, the distinction is just this: where events are frequent and not of any great moment, arrangements for them may undergo a continuous and often unconsidered process of innovation, by modification and drift. But for the major and infrequent, the role of tradition and precedent is bound to be greater. The cake which retains old forms is the cake which is not only evolving more slowly but is doing so with more reference to the past than the mass of frivolous new forms which dance away from it. But where something new and distinctive becomes available, such as piping and tiering and pillars, the past is, for a time until the new possibilities are played out, no longer needed. The new makes special.

Emulation: class, status and origination

A major phenomenon which is unrepresented in the history of the cake, or possibly just hinted at in responses to the putting of cake through rings, is the imposition of change by authority. According to Gillis (1985: 135 ff.), in the century or so before 1850 'bethrothal and wedding had become [in England] the subject of passionate controversy, an issue not so much of religion as of class'. Amongst the lower classes wedding might still be a public matter, an affair for the community in which the young associates of those marrying would have a central role. The propertied classes were however seeking to control marriage, bringing the whole process into the direct control of the family. From the choice of spouse to the conduct of the day itself everything should be done in accordance with the wealth, standing and respectability of the families concerned. From the late eighteenth century, representatives of the upper classes dealing with the common people – parson, squire and master – might campaign to eliminate practices they regarded as unseemly. No doubt this happened sporadically according to character and circumstance, but its effects were cumulative and, ultimately, general. Gillis reports the process as proceeding more quickly in the south and east, so quickly indeed that the record is slight; it was in the north and west where the process was longer drawn out and generated battles over proper songs, the garter, contests and merriment of any kind around the church, of which a record is preserved. In this period there were therefore sharp class differences in the celebration of weddings and at times a direct pressure from the agents of the upper classes to eliminate aspects of older traditions, in effect to propagate their own.

Cake-breaking belonged within the pattern of marrying which was ultimately eliminated, though there is no evidence that in itself it excited any opposition. In the story of the wedding cake it is the alternative phenomenon more characteristic of the succeeding period which has been conspicuous. Hobsbawm (1983b: 306) has noted the strength of emulation in the stratified societies of Europe in the period before the First World War. In a stratified society practices may be identified as relevant to the social status of those performing them. Those lower in the scale may identify with those higher by taking up such practices, to the extent that they have the resources to do so; conversely, they may avoid practices which have become stigmatised.

In the seventeenth century it was in the upper reaches of society that the plum cake developed. As its real cost decreased with an increasing availability of its exotic ingredients and, much later, an enlarging scale of commercial production, so versions became accessible to wider sections of the population. Increasingly over a period of two-and-a-half centuries it was taken up throughout society. It became a familiar and, for weddings, necessary item of British culture despite being, as something to be eaten, by no means universally liked. Starting rather later, in the nineteenth century the royal example was important in establishing the ideal of an elaborately decorated, high-rising cake,[2] though commercial development was needed both for the establishment of the three-tier standard and for it to be possible to emulate it by degrees. A relatively simple, single-tier cake, commercially produced, was a starting point, already a token of the grandest. In the twentieth century, with increasing wealth more and more would be able to attain it more fully.

Innovation has not, however, always been established from the top in this way. In an earlier age the evidence suggests that the 'great cakes' which began the association of cake and wedding originated amongst country and small-town folk. They entered the upper reaches of society only when they could take on the richness of the plum cake as it was being established in the seventeenth century. Similarly, though royalty retained sugarpaste architecture for their official wedding cakes throughout the nineteenth century, they also had other, more personal cakes. These responded from wedding to wedding as the century wore on to the movements of form and style amongst the Queen's subjects, though necessarily only the more affluent. Again, the cutting of the cake which has become so significant in the twentieth century had its roots in the urban middle classes of the nineteenth, before progressing through the entire society, upwards as well as downwards in the social scale. Emulation of practices identified as of high status has therefore been important in shaping the choices which have determined the progress of the cake, but it is far from being a single key to unlock the whole complex course of events.

Centre–periphery and survivals

'Survivals' have been unpopular in anthropology since the displacement of the evolutionism of the nineteenth century by the functionalism of the twentieth. The earlier style depended on sophisticated argument from supposed survivals in order to construct an ultimately discrediting variety of accounts of the past. In the study of cultural change, however, just as it is impossible to miss the way in which innovations often move down, and occasionally up, the social scale, so a clear phenomenon to record is the way they not only move outwards from centres to peripheries but may there often persist, a kind of geographical marooning, long after the originating centres have moved on. This could indeed be said to be what happened to British royal ritual, the plum cake and the tiered, royal-iced wedding cake itself, a European pièce montée petrified into a new age. They survived in Britain with changed significance as the rest of Europe moved on to other possibilities. Similarly with food specialities: the haggis, oatcake, bannock and other Scottish specialities represent in the modern world dishes which are

ancient, were once widespread but which have been maintained in
Scotland as tastes and technology elsewhere moved on.

These are instances which show that the identification of centres and
peripheries, and of survival and innovation, depends on the scale one
chooses. Nevertheless it is clear that there have been cultural leaders
and cultural followers defined geographically. As far as cake-breaking as
a marriage rite is concerned it is, as we have seen, not clear where or even
when it began. What is clear is that it continued in certain areas
relatively remote from centres in which practices which were going to
replace it were already long established. It did not, it is important to
remember, survive inertly – at the end at least, it had diverged in a range
of locally developed traditions – but it was finally replaced by altogether
different patterns rooted primarily in the south of England. There were
times when other areas contributed importantly: Mrs Raffald's
Manchester in the eighteenth century, Chester in the north of England
– known once as the capital of wedding confectionery – for a time in the
nineteenth, Scotland distinctive in various ways at all periods. But all
these were feeding off and feeding into what was to become in the early
twentieth century a common British practice with its basis, like everything else, in the commercial world of the major urban centres. But even
in the era of mass culture and mass media, cake banners in Campbel-
town and wedding shortbread in Shetland were small reminders that the
days of survivals may not have altogether passed.

Changing marriage and changing cakes

For as long as we have any record there have always been two
inconsistent strands in British wedding practices. There has been the
definition of the situation carried by Christian ritual and theology.[3] This
has seen marriage as a relationship entered into by two equivalent
people for their own mutual benefit. Each would be committing
themselves to a different married role as defined by gender, but for both
it was new and different. Popular thinking has however usually regarded
marriage as something done by a man to a woman and essentially about
change for her. Popular marriage rites, as opposed to religious ones,
have therefore commonly focussed on the bride. Only gradually, and
paradoxically with rather more insistence in the most recent period
which many would regard as post-Christian, has the ancient Christian
theme of equivalence begun to make more of a showing. By the 1970s
the term 'symmetrical' was beginning to be applied by observers of
mainly working-class change, to 'the modern pattern' of marriage
(Gorer 1971) and to family trends (Young & Wilmott 1973), but the

ritual change we have observed suggests that in the middle classes it was happening much earlier.

The longer story is complicated however by a retreat from the public celebration of marriage in the eighteenth and nineteenth centuries, not in society at large but amongst many of those best placed to celebrate lavishly. The roots and the reasons for this are various and complex (Gillis 1985: 135 ff.). At an early stage privacy was sought as an aspect of emerging stratification, with respectability requiring that domestic and marital affairs should not be exposed to the gaze, let alone the involvement, of the lower orders. With this went, as has already been noted, the taking over of weddings by families. Marriage was to be accomplished from the bosom of the family, and as the sense of sexual taboo heightened in the nineteenth century, this made marrying an increasingly uneasy process. Perkin (1989: 276) notes that amongst the middle classes 'sex was civilised by ignoring it', but the implication of sexual activity was only too apparent in getting married. It was indeed constantly reiterated in the robust sixteenth-century language which the Church of England persisted in using for its marriage service; Church of Scotland marriages could be more tactful. Though the taboos themselves ensure that the feeling would rarely be recorded in any way, the potentially uncomfortable nature of marrying is clear. The embarrassed couple, the only ones not enjoying their wedding breakfast, were encountered in Chapter 8 above. To this problem the white wedding, as an expression of the cult of bridal purity, provided a partial solution.[4] Even with its distracting aid, respectable young ladies might be expected hardly to be able to face their wedding; rapid departure on a wedding journey, previously undertaken in company if at all but increasingly in the nineteenth century a private honeymoon, would be essential.[5]

This then is one major context of the story we have been tracing. Cakes for breaking belong clearly in the earlier world in which they were playing a part in a palpable rite of passage for the bride, with her bridegroom nowhere in sight. This was something done to her by others, an assertion if you will of the far from private transition she was making. She had a new role to take up in family and in society and it was a role which success in life required all young females to achieve. Each bride was therefore special, and would remain so as long as becoming a bride remained crucial for female lives. The taking of pieces of broken cake, or cake passed through the wedding ring, or cake cut – indeed at various times of other items associated closely with the bride – on which to dream has its long-running basis here.

It is in cake-cutting however that the historical transition is clearly marked. What began as a sheerly practical task, to be performed by servants or whoever might be available, became in the mid-nineteenth century a respectable role for the bride to perform as dispenser of cake to the assembled families. The bride was to make a timid first assertion, in a safe idiom, of her role as an active participant, if not yet an initiator, in the process of marrying. We have seen the development of the cutting as a rite increasingly divorced from the practical preparation of cake for eating. It was thereby prepared for the new rationale as inauguration which was to be attached to it. It was still the bride who was to perform it, but the twentieth-century husband would ultimately come to her aid. The outcome is familiar, a joint action interpreted as an inauguration of jointness. The once passive bride who became first an active participant had finally become half of the equal couple.

As to the style of the wedding cake when it developed, the formality and impersonality of its hard, repetitive, white piped ornamentation, and the cautious and restricted adoption of symbolic devices for it, the appropriateness of this at last begins to emerge. It is a style more puritan than sensuous, a part of that diversionary tactic which was the white wedding.

Postscript

This study has focussed on the wedding cake as it developed in Britain from the seventeenth to the twentieth centuries. It became in that time a familiar part of life for British people and for many others around the world, indeed a part taken for granted. To many more still it and its relationship to marrying became instantly recognisable. In the last decade of the twentieth century its future is, however, a great deal less certain.

As has been discussed, an immediate cause has been the eruption into the wedding-cake trade in Britain of a new set of players. These are enthusiasts who initially learnt their skills as part of the sugarcraft movement and moved on to commercial production of celebration cakes. 'Celebration cakes' has indeed become a new category, uniting two previously contrasted sections of confectioners' production. The distinction between 'novelties' produced mainly for children and inexpensive, and serious and costly cakes for important occasions, of which the wedding cake was certainly the most serious and the most costly, has weakened. On the one hand, fun cakes have spread increasingly into the adult world, particularly in the context of public and media inaugurations, on the other the 'serious' cakes have begun to retreat from the formality which has marked their seriousness since the rise of the white wedding cake.

The old formula, the set of three tiers of declining size mounted vertically with pillars between the tiers, becomes now an option or a theme on which to construct variations. New icing and the new styles of decoration which go along with them may be used to construct the old standard form but equally they may suggest something new. American or Victorian examples may be called on for stacked cakes without pillars, but stands on which the tiers will be presented separately have also appeared. The cakes may then be displayed either in the old configuration one above the other or they may be variously offset. They may also be mounted separately, three cakes of different size but still matching, set up on separated stands at different heights, the largest lowest. These are all manifest variations on the old theme, for a time at which the old formula is still clearly in everyone's mind. They may not last; we have already seen more radical possibilities emerging. We noted the set of three cakes of identical size mounted to form a set of steps and decorated not as scaled versions one of the other but in accordance with the theme, of steps with bride and groom at their head. This was being offered not by some consciously innovative individual confectioner but by a popular and long-established wedding-cake manufacturer. We have also seen the rising demand for single-tier cakes. A new cake book published in 1990 included the suggestion for a single-tier wedding cake with a hole in its centre in which could repose a bottle of champagne. More significantly, a couple each with children from a previous marriage were presented with a sugarpaste cake surmounted by a delightful model in natural colours of themselves together on a settee with their new combined family perched around them. The old order was showing signs of breaking up.

The most direct source of such innovations was, as has been discussed, the new style developed in Australia. This was a direct development out of the tradition it is now subverting. As such it can be readily seen, and indeed is seen, not as a distinctive Australian cake but as a new version of the standard. At the same time, there is increasing interest in Britain in forms the distinctive origins of which are indeed part of their attraction. One bride may insist on 'an American shower cake', identified as a stacked cake decorated with cascades of sugar rosebuds down its sides; another may have set her heart on the French croquembouche style. There was, that is to say, both an increasing awareness of alternatives and a growing sense that a wedding cake might be any one of a number of different things. By the early 1990s the effect here was still marginal, but increasing mobility within a unifying Europe seemed bound to support the trend.

And marriage itself: is this changing? From being one of the major foundations for the organisation of life and for social and physical reproduction, it is progressing towards being no more than a personal and optional contract. If the process continues, then it will hardly be surprising if the collective and impersonal significances which have previously shaped the cake's evolution give way. New and more personal cakes for celebrating new marriages, never again to be so standardised, may be the new order gradually displacing 'the old tradition' in the nooks and crannies of the land. Or perhaps, though this as yet hardly bears thinking, there may be no wedding cakes at all.

Notes

INTRODUCTION

1 The title of the section of her essays in which her treatment of the wedding cake is published is 'Food as a system of communication' (Douglas 1982: 82 ff.). This is to echo Barthes's pioneering essay of 1961: 'For what is food? It is not only a collection of products that can be used for statistical or nutritional studies. It is also, and at the same time, a system of communication, a body of images, a protocol of usages, situations, and behaviour' (Barthes 1979: 167). It is perhaps characteristic of the enterprise that none of the direct and obvious uses of food are mentioned here. Despite Douglas's title, the communication aspect of the structuralist programme is not prominent in her analysis of this topic; her goal is an underlying system governing behaviour. Cf. Mintz 1985: 200.

1 THE BRITISH WEDDING CAKE IN THE LATE TWENTIETH CENTURY

1 This account concentrates on professionally made cakes. Evidence from a survey carried out in 1982/3 for *Wedding Day and First Home*, a bridal magazine, suggested that professional cakes were most likely in Scotland and the Borders (69 per cent) and least likely in Northern Ireland (27 per cent) and the North East of England (24 per cent). The range recorded elsewhere was between 44 and 58 per cent. Scotland and the Borders also recorded the highest average expenditure on the cake, £61, against £53 for the United Kingdom as a whole.

2 HOW DISTINCTIVE IS THE BRITISH WEDDING CAKE?

1 British recipes were sometimes reprinted rather directly as American. The Raffald cake appears for example in Miss F.'s *American Home Confectionery Book* (1888) and Francatelli's in Anon. 1866.
2 Seligson (1974: 98), a journalist writing on the American wedding industry, comments: 'What we think of today as the wedding cake is actually the "bride's cake" – frilly, decorative, not meant to be eaten. The "groom's cake"

was dark, a fruitcake, practical, substantial. The sexist implications rise like the yeast.'

3 'Frosting' is an alternative term to 'icing' often used in the United States. It seems first to have been applied to pulverised sugar, perhaps with starch added to reduce caking, when this began to be manufactured commercially in the mid-nineteenth century. American interest in icings/frostings has typically been greater than British; a far wider range is generally offered by American cookery books than by British.

4 From an item in *The New York Times*, 10 June 1987, describing wedding cakes destined for a window display at Tiffany, New York. Cutting kindly supplied by Bridget Ann Henisch.

5 Developments in Australia deserve far more attention than I have been able to give them here, despite valuable assistance and leads kindly provided by Barbara Santich of the University of Adelaide.

6 Edwards (1982: 700, 709) provides a more detailed commentary. He suggests *inter alia* that the two cakes may in fact have had western origins and that their use was therefore less creative than Wilson believed. More evidence is required.

7 His earlier work had put the starting point in the 1920s. It also provides a discussion of symbolism. He argues that such cultural adoption 'is not simply a question of "what catches the imagination", but rather, given the range of forms that historically contingent factors produce, which of those forms *could* catch the imagination' (Edwards 1982: 709, 700).

3 CULTURAL CREATION: MYTH, HISTORY AND LANGUAGE

1 Seligson (1974: 97) extends the myth interestingly: she assumes that the cakes would be numerous and would therefore stack high 'in front of the newly weds'. An ordeal was thus set up: 'the custom was for the couple to try to kiss over the mound; if successful, they were thus assured of lifelong prosperity and endless children.' See Chapter 4, notes 7 and 8 below.

4 WHEN THE WEDDING CAKE WAS NOT YET AND MIGHT NEVER HAVE BEEN

1 An excellent general account of the history of baking and of cakes is provided by Wilson 1973. The somewhat disordered way in which I came to the present research meant that I encountered it only when much of my own basic research had been done. I was much encouraged to find, nevertheless, that my own conclusions did not differ greatly from those of so clear an expert.

2 It may usefully be compared with the wedding feasts amongst the Parisian bourgeoisie of a hundred years earlier detailed by *Le Ménagier de Paris* (Power 1928: 238–47). There are a number of puzzles here and a commentary by a suitably qualified historian is clearly required. Henisch (1976: 232–3) provides the only comment I have found, on one of the subtleties. This is quoted in the text below.

3 According to Hieatt & Butler (1985: 4–5), the first course in a medieval feast was the everyday basic meal. Subsequent courses were a succession of

reduplications. Later courses would include greater delicacies, but whether participants were entitled to partake would depend on their rank. Only the highest would be offered everything.

4 The editor suggests this should be something to do with 'seoir' (French) to sit. The text was published from a copy of uncertain accuracy from a contemporary manuscript not itself available at the time.

5 = girdle, a flat iron plate suspended over a fire and still used in Scotland for soda or girdle scones and dropped scones or Scotch pancakes.

6 This refers to Jesus' miraculous conversion of water into wedding wine (St John 2).

7 The picture to which he refers was published in the Genevan Bible of 1560 and copied in versions printed in England later in the century. 'Shewbread' was the twelve loaves displayed in the Jewish Temple and renewed each Sabbath. Rounded, flat loaves or cakes, perhaps six inches in diameter, are shown in two columns of six, one cake on top of another. They rest on a dish of somewhat greater diameter, and there is an ornamented cover of the same size on the top. Aubrey makes just the same comment on the piling up in Shropshire of 'Soule-cakes' for All Souls' Day. These were 'about the bigness of 2d. cakes, and n'ly all the visitants that day take one' (Aubrey 1881: 23). The reference to such a picture makes it clear not only that there were a number of cakes but that they were round and flat enough to be piled up.

8 Herrick's Julia would have been one such. See also his poem, 'To the Maids to Walk abroad'. I have found no warrant for going beyond this to Jeaffreson's assertion that the cakes were plural because the guests had each baked and brought one along. Laneham's three and even Aubrey's shewbread analogy do not suggest any such thing unless very small wedding parties are to be envisaged. See also Chapter 3, note 1 above.

9 If a functional equivalent had been sought, *Mustaceum*, a Roman wedding cake of unfermented wine and flour, would probably have been chosen (Soyer 1853: 286; Lewis & Short 1879).

10 *OED* refers to mythical transparent stones in cocks' gizzards, but testicles are more likely here, as for the lambs which follow. See *OED*: stone.

11 The 'four and twenty blackbirds baked in a pie', of the nursery rhyme, perpetuate the memory of such entertainments. They are recorded as having actually appeared at the Burgundian court in the fifteenth century. The same idea but applied to cakes reappeared in the twentieth century in America (Seligson 1974: 101).

5 GREAT CAKES, PLUM(B) CAKES AND BRIDE CAKES

1 There seems to be little evidence from which to document the history of pastry-cooks, beyond the flourishing of fashionable establishments in London in the eighteenth century: see Davis 1966; Mui & Mui 1989. They re-enter our story in the guise of 'confectioners' in the nineteenth century: see Chapter 7 below.

2 *The Boston Cooking-School Cook Book* offered something more ambitious however. Apart from molasses and squares of melted chocolate listed as standard ingredients, the possibility of adding a pint of preserved strawberries was suggested. This was as an addition to an already elaborate spiced, rich-fruit mixture (Farmer 1949: 688).

3 This was sent out with Marchant 1879, which work they themselves published.

6 CONFECTIONERY AND ICING

1 A printer's error in Mrs Glasse's first edition jumbles two very different icing recipes under the single heading 'To Ice a great Cake another way'. By the third edition both the original recipes had been abandoned. It has not been possible to consult the second edition.

2 For a claimed Swiss-German origin of meringue as such in 1720, see Montagné 1961: 620.

3 It is an interesting pointer to the difficulty of avoiding preconceptions and jumping to conclusions on the basis of them not only that Jeaffreson was able to get matters so wrong but that the present author was for so long unable to register the kind of thing to which his predecessor had been referring.

4 See Littlewood (Part 2) 1989, who reproduces it from 'old prints and drawings'.

5 This was soon put into circulation in the United States, appearing verbatim in Anon. 1866.

6 It is tempting to imagine that recent techniques of symbolic analysis would be able to extract a variety of meanings from the patterns used and the way they changed over time (see below). While this may not be impossible, the precedents are so far not encouraging: see, e.g., Sinclair 1987. Unlike the designs on pots or silverware, there is the added difficulty here that examples of piped ornamentation do not remain physically available to be sampled and analysed.

7 Experimentation in styles of decoration did continue in the twentieth century. Nirvana (1951; 1954) worked hard to develop and popularise the technique which he called 'run-in' and which has subsequently come to be known as 'run-out' or 'flood-in'. This involves outlining a design by piping onto waxed paper, then filling in the shape with runny royal icing and building it up with further piping as required. When the piece has hardened it can be removed from the paper and attached to the cake. Nirvana produced large and distinctive plates and collars for the tops of cakes, and for square cakes might even cover the sides with 'run-in' plates rather than conventional royal icing. Though this work had little impact on the old piped style in general use, it did contribute to the resources which would be available to the cake decorator when more radical change began in the 1980s.

7 THE RISE OF THE VICTORIAN CAKE AND ITS SUCCESSORS

1 For an account of his shop, displaying Twelfth cakes, the star turn of the confectionery trade before the wedding cake took over, see Sandys 1833: lxxvii, and Henisch 1984: 142–3.

2 While all the 'compartments' were in white, the picture suggests that this was not true of all the decoration. Apparently white medallions on the base seem to have been set on a coloured ground.

3 This appears to show an intention to cut up the cake, but since there were only four medallions it is not clear exactly what was intended.

4 R. Bolland & Sons, of Eastgate Street, Chester, were Confectioners by Appointment to Queen Victoria and the Prince of Wales, afterwards Edward VII. They were for a considerable period the leading wedding-cake manufacturers in the country.

5 This is not to say that there had not been other tiered cakes by this time. Weaver (1990) reprints a Kentucky recipe of 1848 for a fruit pound cake arranged in layers in a pyramid, and from Australia there exists a wedding-breakfast photograph of 1861 apparently displaying an elaborate three-tier cake (Newton 1988: 22). The picture is, however, heavily retouched and it is impossible to tell the nature of the upper tiers.

6 For an account of cakes at twentieth-century royal weddings, see Laverack 1979: 117–20. It will be noted that she is a late follower of the Jeaffreson theory of the origin of the wedding cake. Cannadine (1983) charts the growth of state ritual in Britain and the place of the monarchy in it. The record of royal wedding cakes and of media attention to them fits with his emphasis on the last quarter of the nineteenth century as the period of major development. It also, however, shows attention gradually building up in the preceding decades.

7 In the bread and flour confectionery trades in general, this was a period of great innovation as mechanisation began to be applied: 'invention followed invention' (Jefferys 1954: 211). For examples of the use of the wedding cake, see Vine 1894; Lewis & Bromley 1903.

8 The work was originally *The Confectioner's Handbook and Practical Sugar Boiler*.

9 Separate tiers are also advantageous for transport. Unlike a stacked cake, decorated overall, tiers can be boxed separately and assembled at the site of the wedding.

10 This idea could be taken further. A well-known authority on cake decorating and sugarcraft suggested 'incorporating the actual lace used for the wedding dress or veil of the bride into the design of the cake', and gave instructions for doing it. This would make it a 'personal wedding cake' (Wallace 1975: 160).

11 The Victorian enthusiasm for flowers as decoration is discussed by Jameson (1987: 61–2) in his valuable account of the ritual of the dinner party.

12 In the following chapter he describes the same cake as looking like 'an ill-soldered silver castle'. It was for a wedding conducted in a pretentious style of which the narrator is represented as disapproving.

8 USES AND THEIR EVOLUTION

1 The possibility of slicing bread and the superiority of slicing to breaking are old however: see Henisch 1976: 155–61.

2 He slips from one term to the other in a way that denies the presence of any fundamental distinction.

3 The north-east was an area in which Catholic pockets survived. It is possible therefore that the bridal bread continued to have a religious setting there after its abolition elsewhere.

4 His work, following most notably Ben Jonson (1616, see edition of 1941), was steeped in a fascination for the rites and ceremonies of the ancient world,

mediated often by continental scholars of the previous century, such as Giraldi, Brisson and Hotman. The possibilities of classical influence or even direct quotation, as worked out by generations of literary scholars (Martin 1956; Braden 1978), have therefore to be taken into account before the apparently ethnographic evidence of his work can be accepted.

5 The 'bride's bonn' has however been recorded as continuing in Shetland into the twentieth century. By then it was a rich caraway shortbread, broken but not over the bride's head. The pieces were kept in a sieve which was at one point held over her head. Later they would be taken away for dreaming (Mackay 1987).

6 Van Gennep (1909) drew attention first to the number of 'passages' which occur in life, movements personal or collective from one state to another. He found a pattern to the mass of apparently strange actions which people around the world perform in connection with such passages. It is a pattern with three parts to it, of which the second is the most interesting and has proved most theoretically stimulating. First there are rites of separation which make the passage out of the pre-existing state; then there are liminal rites which hold those concerned in an exceptional, extra-normal state, of which being a bride is a rather typical example; and finally there are rites which make the return to normality but in a new capacity, of wife for instance. Van Gennep's theory is far more interesting but less well known than the term he originated. See also pp. 24 above.

7 It has not been possible to trace this source, hence the date is unknown. As with all such works used here, it is impossible to know the extent to which the author is reporting an existing practice or campaigning for one.

8 A small silver coin. It was the silver threepence, half its size, which was subsequently used in the middle of the twentieth century in Christmas puddings, not as divination but simply as treasure to be found.

9 By the 1870s, in London at least it might be provided by caterers. Messrs Hill offered menus and all requirements except the cake at between 11s 6d and 17s. 6d. a head, or £1 with real turtle soup. The basis here was a buffet, to which one further hot course was to be added at each higher price (Marchant 1879).

10 The 'former déjeuner with its long tables, speechifying, and array of meats' was being replaced by an afternoon tea, albeit supplemented with 'champagne and claret-cup' by the turn of the century. For the upper classes it may well have been going out even earlier (Anon. 1902; Jalland 1986: 36). As commonly happens with well-established social practices however, it took a long time adying. Monsarrat (1973: 189) is able to assert that full-blown wedding breakfasts went out of favour with the Second World War.

11 The difficulty had already been noted by Willy in the 1890s (1891: 53), as well as the saw and pre-cutting beneath the icing as solutions.

12 For the ultimate and effective cutting, the cake might be unceremoniously upended, to be sliced more easily from the uniced bottom (Lock 1990: 125).

13 For the latter it is noted that it was no longer to be served separately, but 'judiciously mixed in small pieces with other varieties of cake' (Anon. 1902: 76–7). A little rite was being made out of this too.

9 MEANINGS AND INTERPRETATION

1 Or even for divorce. A Scottish handbook used a torn photograph of wedding-cake cutting as its cover picture (Nichols 1978).

2 From the sixteen out of sixty sufficiently interested to reply came the richest set of extra meanings obtained. The harvest of replies was exiguous to non-existent from London and the south of England, generous from the north. The following discussion is based on this material, supplemented by earlier findings and with occasional reference back to older sources.

3 This was almost certainly doomed to failure. Shaw & Chase (1989: 4) argue that nostalgia requires the evidences of the past to be physically present. The sense in which this can be true of any food item, even the wedding cake, is probably too indirect to form an adequate anchor.

4 But it could be that, for this respondent, the cut stands for sex which stands for union: see below.

5 The same author asserts elsewhere (1989 (Part 3): 24), 'The most popular shape of bride cake is the round one, this being symbolic of eternity, although square cakes have become increasingly popular in recent years, probably because they are easier to cut into slices.' This is to imply that the symbolic is somehow effective, though not to the extent of counteracting practical advantage. If anyone were incautious enough to assert straightforwardly that the shape was popular because of its symbolic significance, this would invite immediate rebuttal.

10 TOWARDS A THEORY OF CULTURAL CHANGE?

1 Also used by Nutt (1789: 46) in a commercial cake, a very special two-guinea cake. It may well have been intended for wedding use though he does not say so.

2 As it was in promoting new styles of carriage, through the same period (Cannadine 1983: 112).

3 For a discussion of the nature of Christian marriage, its development and its relationship to popular rites, and for relevant references, see my *Rites of Marrying* (1991).

4 The history of the white wedding has not, despite Monsarrat's useful compilation (1973), been seriously researched. It was a development many of the components of which had long been available. A symbolic meaning attached to white, white dresses and veils for brides, and white-iced cakes had all been possible long before they were welded into a pattern of compelling coherence in the later nineteenth century. Its apparent logic then favoured the exclusion of colour generally. White favours and a worldwide search for white flowers – even at times the extinction of their green foliage – and menfolk dressed only in black and white resulted.

5 'Honeymoon', as documented by the *OED* and Stone (1977: 334–6), is a term of considerable interest. In the sixteenth and seventeenth centuries it referred to the initial fullness of marital enthusiasm and its expected rapid waning. This was not a concept likely to receive much support in the Romantic age to follow. There is little documentation for the term from the eighteenth century, but in the nineteenth it reappears in the very different sense still familiar, i.e. for a time away after the wedding. The metaphorical and, one might say, insightful meaning of the term, which might be imagined

to be derivative from the more concrete and banal, is therefore historically primary. As concerns privacy, it may be that going away without company has its origins as a social practice more in the lack of resources to do otherwise amongst the enlarging middle classes than in any search for it. Jalland (1986: 41–2) shows that Stone's account is inadequate, at least in its chronology and at least for the upper classes.

Bibliography

ABBREVIATIONS

BB   British Baker
CC   Chester Chronicle
ILN   Illustrated London News
OED Oxford English Dictionary, Compact Edition 1971, Oxford: Oxford
    University Press.

Acton, E. (1873) *Modern Cookery for Private Families*, new edn, London:
    Longmans. (First published 1845.)
Agrestis (1818) 'Sketches of Scottish scenery and manners', *Edinburgh Magazine*:
    409–15.
Alexis (1558) *Secretes of the Reverende Maister Alexis of Piedmont*, London.
Anon. (1854) *Etiquette, Social Ethics and the Courtesies of Society*, London: Orr.
Anon. (1866) *The Art of Confectionery*, Boston: Tilton.
Anon. (1880) *Etiquette of Good Society*, London: Cassell.
Anon. (1902) *Etiquette of Marriage*, London: John Macqueen.
Art-Journal (1851) *The Crystal Palace Exhibition*, London. (Reprinted New
    York: Dover, 1970.)
Aubrey, J. (1881) *The Remaines of Gentilisme and Judaisme*, London: Satchell,
    Peyton for Folk-lore Society. (First published 1686–7.)
Austin, T. (ed.) (1888) *Two Fifteenth-Century Cookery Books*, London: Early
    English Text Society.
Baillie, J. (1851) *The Dramatic and Poetical Works*, London: Longman, Brown.
Baker, M. (1977) *Wedding Customs and Folklore*, Newton Abbot: David &
    Charles.
Baret, J. (1580) *An Alvearie or Quadruple Dictionarie*, augmented edn, London.
Barth, F. (1977) *Ritual and Knowledge among the Baktaman of New Guinea*,
    Oslo: Universitetsforlaget.
—— (1989) 'The analysis of culture in complex societies', *Ethnos* 54: 120–42.
Barthes, R. (1979) 'Towards a psychosociology of food and consumption', in R.
    Foster and O. Ranum (eds) *Food and Drink in History*, Baltimore: Johns
    Hopkins University Press.
Bauer, F. (1924) *Cake-Art-Craft*, Chicago: Bauer.
Beaumont, F. and Fletcher, J. (1616) *The Scornful Lady*, London. (Reprinted

in Bowers, F. (ed.) *The Dramatic Works in the Beaumont and Fletcher Canon*, Cambridge: Cambridge University Press, 1970.)

Becker, H. (1982) *Art Worlds*, Berkeley: University of California Press.

Bee, M. and Bee, S. (1935) *Weddings Without Worry*, London: Methuen.

Beeton, I. (1861) *The Book of Household Management*, London: Beeton.

—— (1872) *Beeton's Every-day Cookery and Housekeeping Book*, London: Ward Lock.

—— (1923) *The Book of Household Management* (and previous and subsequent edns), London: Ward Lock.

Bennion, E.B. and Stewart, J. (1945) *Cake Making*, 3rd edn, London: Hill.

Borella (1770) *The Court and Country Confectioner*, London. (New edn 1772.)

Braden, G. (1978) 'Herrick's classical quotations', in R.B. Rollin and J.M. Patrick (eds) *'Trust to good verses': Herrick Tercentenary Essays*, Pittsburgh: Pittsburgh University Press.

Brears, P. (1987) *Traditional Food in Yorkshire*, Edinburgh: Donald.

Caird, J. (1809) *The Complete Confectioner and Family Cook*, Leith.

Cannadine, D. (1983) 'The context, performance and meaning of ritual: the British monarchy and the "invention of tradition", c. 1820–1977', in E. Hobsbawm and T. Ranger (eds) *The Invention of Tradition*, Cambridge: Cambridge University Press.

Carême, A. (1828) *Le Pâtissier Royal Parisien*, 2 vols, 10th edn, Paris.

Carr, W. (1828) *The Dialect of Craven in the West Riding of the County of Yorkshire*, 2 vols, 2nd edn, London: Crofts.

Charsley, S.R. (1987a) 'Interpretation and custom: the case of the wedding cake', *Man* (N.S.) 22: 93–110.

—— (1987b) 'What does a wedding cake mean?', *New Society* 81, 3 July: 11–14.

—— (1988) 'The wedding cake: history and meanings', *Folklore* 99: 232–41.

—— (1991) *Rites of Marrying: the Wedding Industry in Scotland*, Manchester: Manchester University Press.

Cordon Bleu (1893) *British Baker* X: 587.

Cox, G. (1903) *The Art of Confectionery*, Birmingham: National Association of Master Bakers and Confectioners.

Dalrymple, G. (1781) *Practice of Modern Cookery*, Edinburgh.

Daniel, A.R. (1978) *Up-to-date Confectionery*, 4th edn, London: Applied Science. (First edn 1936.)

Davies, F. (1892) *Cakes and Biscuits*, London: Virtue.

Davis, D. (1966) *A History of Shopping*, London: Routledge & Kegan Paul.

Dekker, T. (1602) *Satiro-mastix*, London.

Deloney, T. (1912) *The Works of Thomas Deloney*, ed. F.O. Mann, Oxford: Clarendon Press.

Derraugh, P. and Derraugh, W. (1983) *Wedding Etiquette*, London: Foulsham.

Dickens, C. (1846) *The Cricket on the Hearth*, London: Bradbury & Evans. (Penguin edn 1971.)

—— (1853) *Bleak House*, London: Chapman and Hall.

Digbie, K. (1669) *The Closet of the Eminently Learned Sir Kenelme Digbie Kᵗ Opened*, London.

Dods, M. (1826) *The Cook and Housewife's Manual* (and subsequent edns), Edinburgh: Oliver & Boyd.

Dolby, R. (1830) *Cook's Dictionary and Housekeeper's Directory*, London: Colburn & Bentley.

Douglas, M. (1975) 'Deciphering a meal', in her *Implicit Meanings*, London: Routledge & Kegan Paul.

—— (1982) 'Food as an art form', in her *In the Active Voice*, London: Routledge & Kegan Paul.

—— (ed.) (1984) *Food in the Social Order*, New York: Russell Sage Foundation.

Douglas, M. and Nicod, M. (1974) 'Taking the biscuit: the structure of British meals', *New Society* 33: 744–7.

Doyle, R. (1850) *Manners and Customs of ye Englyshe*, vol. 2, London: Bradbury & Evans.

—— (1885) *A Journal Kept by Richard Doyle in the Year 1840*, London: Smith, Elder.

Eales, M. (1718) *Mrs Mary Eales' Receipts*, London.

Edwards, W.D. (1982) 'Something borrowed: wedding cakes as symbols in modern Japan', *American Ethnologist* 9: 699–711.

—— (1984) 'Ritual in the Commercial World: Japanese Society through its Weddings', unpublished PhD thesis, Cornell University.

Emmison, F.G. (1964) *Tudor Food and Pastimes*, London: Benn.

F., Miss (1888) *American Home Confectionery Book*, Paris: Guillard.

Farmer, F.M. (1911) *Catering for Special Occasions*, Philadelphia: McKay.

—— (1949) *The Boston Cooking-School Cook Book*, London: Harrap. (Reprint of 8th edn of 1946.)

Fieldhouse, P. (1986) *Food and Nutrition: Customs and Culture*, London: Croom Helm.

Firth, R. (1973) 'Food symbolism', in his *Symbols Public and Private*, London: Allen & Unwin.

Francatelli, C.E. (1862) *The Royal English and Foreign Confectioner*, London: Chapman and Hall.

Frazer, Mrs (1791) *Practice of Cookery, Pastry, Pickling, Preserving, etc.*, Edinburgh: Hill.

—— (1806) *Practice of Cookery, Pastry and Confectionery*, 5th edn, Edinburgh: Hill.

—— (1820) *Practice of Cookery, Pastry and Confectionary*, 7th edn, Edinburgh: Frazer.

Frese, P.R. (1982) 'Holy Matrimony: a Symbolic Analysis of American Wedding Ritual', unpublished PhD thesis, Univerity of Virginia.

Furnivall, F.J. (ed.) (1868) *Early English Meals and Manners*, London: Early English Text Society.

Garine, I.L. de (1976) 'Food, tradition, and prestige', in D.N. Walcher *et al.* (eds) *Food, Man, and Society*, New York: Plenum.

Gillis, J.R. (1985) *For Better, for Worse: British Marriages, 1600 – Present*, New York: Oxford University Press.

Glasse, H. (1747) *The Art of Coookery Made Plain and Easy*, London. (3rd edn 1755.)

—— (1760) *The Compleat Confectioner*, London.

Gommez, R. (1895) *Piping and Ornamentation*, London: Baker & Confectioner.

—— (1896) *Cakes, Gateaux and Biscuits*, London: Hampton.

—— (1899) *Cake Decoration: Flower and Classic Piping*, London: Baker & Confectioner.

Good Housekeeping (1989) 135: 6.

Goode, J.G., Curtis, K. and Theophano, J. (1984) 'Meal formats, meal cycles, and menu negotiation in the maintenance of an Italian-American community', in M. Douglas (ed.) *Food in the Social Order*, New York: Russell Sage Foundation.

Goody, J. (1982) *Cooking, Cuisine and Class*, Cambridge: Cambridge University Press.

Gorer, G. (1971) *Sex and Marriage in England Today*, London: Nelson.

Gouffé, A. (1874) *The Royal Book of Pastry and Confectionery*, London: Sampson Low.

Grant, I.F. (1961) *Highland Folk Ways*, London: Routledge & Kegan Paul.

Gregor, W. (1881) *Notes on the Folk-lore of the North-east of Scotland*, London: Folk-lore Society.

Grey, E. (1935) *Cottage Life in a Hertfordshire Village*, Harpenden: Harpenden and District Local History Society.

Haldane, R. (1883) *Workshop Receipts*, Ser. II, London.

Halkett, A. (1979) *Memoirs*, ed. J. Loftis, Oxford: Clarendon Press.

Hanneman, L.J. (1978) *Modern Cake Decoration*, 2nd edn, London: Applied Science Publishers.

Harland, J. (1867) *Manchester Collectanea*, vol. 2, Manchester: Chetham Society.

Harris, H.G. (1903) *Confectionery Critiques*, London: British Baker.

Henderson, W.A. (1793) *The Housekeeper's Instructor; or, Universal Family Cook*, London: Stratford.

—— (1805) *The Housekeeper's Instructor; or, Universal Family Cook*, 13th edn, London: Stratford.

Henderson, W. (1866) *Notes on the Folk Lore of the Northern Counties of England and the Borders*, London: Longmans.

Henisch, B.A. (1976) *Fast and Feast: Food in Medieval Society*, University Park, Pennsylvania: Pennsylvania State University.

—— (1984) *Cakes and Characters: an English Christmas Tradition*, London: Prospect Books.

Henwood, G. (1972) *Cornwall's Mines and Miners*, Truro: Bradford Barton.

Heritage, L. (1894) *Cassel's New Universal Cookery Book*, London, Cassell.

Herrick, R. (1648) *Hesperides: or, The Works both Humane and Divine of Robert Herrick Esq.*, London.

Hieatt, C.B. and Butler, S. (eds) (1985) *Curye on Inglysch: English Culinary Manuscripts of the Fourteenth Century*, London: Oxford University Press.

Hindley, C. (1878) *The Life and Times of James Catnach, Ballad Monger*, London: Reeves & Turner.

Hobsbawm, E. (1983a) *Introduction*, in E. Hobsbawm and T. Ranger (eds) *The Invention of Tradition*, Cambridge: Cambridge University Press.

—— (1983b) 'Mass-producing traditions: Europe, 1870– 1914', in E. Hobsbaum and T. Ranger (eds) *The Invention of Tradition*, Cambridge: Cambridge University Press.

Houblon, A.A. (1907) *The Houblon Family*, 2 vols, London: Constable.

Howell, J. (1890) In *The Familiar Letters*, ed. J. Jacobs, London: Nutt.

Hueg, H. (1901) *Ornamental Confectionery and the Art of Baking*, 7th edn, New York: Hueg.

Huloet, R. (1552) *Abcedarium Anglico Latinum*, London. (Reprinted Menston: Scolar Press, 1970.)

Hunter, M. (1936) *Reaction to Conquest*, London: Oxford University Press.

Inman, C. (1938) *ABC of Weddings*, London: Blackie.

Jack, F.B. (1907) *Cakes*, London: Jack.

Jalland, P. (1986) *Women, Marriage and Politics*, 1860–1914, Oxford: Clarendon Press.

Jameson, R. (1987) 'Purity and power at the Victorian dinner party', in I. Hodder (ed.), *The Archaeology of Contextual Meanings*, Cambridge: Cambridge University Press.

Jarrin, W.A. (1820) *The Italian Confectioner*, London: Harding.

Jeaffreson, J.C. (1872) *Brides and Bridals*, 2 vols, London: Hurst & Blackett.

Jeanes, W. (1861) *The Modern Confectioner*, London.

Jefferys, J.B. (1954) *Retail Trading in Britain 1850–1950*, Cambridge: Cambridge University Press.

Jones, O. (1856) *The Grammar of Ornament*, London: Day.

Jonson, B. (1616) 'Christmas his Masque', printed in C.H. Herford Percy and E. Simpson (eds) *Ben Jonson*, Oxford: Clarendon Press, 1941.

Keesing, R.M. (1892) 'Introduction' to G. Herdt (ed.) *Rituals of Manhood*, Berkeley: University of California Press.

Kightly, C. (1986) *The Customs and Ceremonies of Britain*, London: Thames & Hudson.

Kirkland, J. (ed.) (1909) *The Modern Baker, Confectioner and Caterer*, vol. V, London: Gresham.

Kitchiner, W. (1823) *The Cook's Oracle*, 5th edn, London: Constable of Edinburgh.

—— (1840) *The Cook's Oracle*, new edn, Edinburgh: Cadell.

La Fontaine, J. (1977) 'The power of rights', *Man* (N.S.) 12: 421–37.

Laneham, R. (1907) *Robert Laneham's letter: describing a part of the Entertainment unto Queen Elizabeth at the Castle of Kenilworth in 1575*, ed. F.J. Furnival, London: Chatto & Windus.

Laverack, E. (1979) *With This Ring: 100 Years of Marriage*, London: Elm Tree Books.

Leach, E.R. (1976) *Culture and Communication*, Cambridge: Cambridge University Press.

Lebra, T.S. (1984) *Japanese Women*, Honolulu: University of Hawaii Press.

Leonard, D. (1980) *Sex and Generation*, London: Tavistock.

Lewis, C.T. and Short, C. (1879) *A Latin Dictionary*, Oxford: Clarendon Press.

Lewis, T.P. and Bromley, A.G. (1903) *The Book of Cakes*, London: Maclaren.

Leyel, Mrs C.F. (1936) *Cakes of England*, London: Routledge.

Little, M. (1929) *The Complete Cake Book*, London: Werner Laurie.

Littlewood, A. (1989) 'Wedding cakes', Part 2 (29 April), Part 3 (13 May), Part 7 (5 August), *British Baker*.

Llewellyn-Davies, M. (1984) *The Women's Olamal* (film), London: BBC.

Lock, P. (1990) *Cake Decorating: An A–Z of Hints and Tips*, London: Merehurst.

Longmate, N. (1971) *How We Lived Then: a History of Everyday Life during the Second World War*, London: Hutchinson.

Macdonald, D. (1812) *The New London Family Cook*, London: Albion Press.

McGregor, D. (ed.) (1905) *The Rathen Manual*, Aberdeen: Aberdeen Ecclesiological Society (Transactions IV, Special Issue).

MacGregor, E. (1988) *Wedding Cakes*, London: Merehurst.

Mackay, M. (1987) 'Food and friends', unpublished conference paper, Glasgow.

McLintock, Mrs (1736) *Mrs McLintock's Receipts for Cookery and Pastry Work*, Glasgow. (Reprinted Aberdeen: Aberdeen University Press, 1986.)

McMillan, W. (1931–2) 'Mediaeval survivals in Scottish worship', *Church Service Society Annual*: 21–34.

Marchant, W.T. (1879) *Betrothals and Bridals, with a Chat about Wedding Cakes and Wedding Customs*, London: Hill.

Markham, G. (1615) *The English House-wife*, London.

Marshall, R.K. (1983) *Virgins and Viragos: a History of Women In Scotland 1080–1980*, London: Collins.

Martin, L.C. (ed.) (1956) *Herrick's Poetical Works*, Oxford: Clarendon Press.

Masson, G. (1966) 'Food as fine art in seventeenth-century Rome', *Apollo*: 338–41.

May, R. (1665) *The Accomplish't Cook: or, the Art and Mystery of Cookery*, 2nd edn, London.

Mennell, S. (1985) *All Manners of Food: Eating and Taste in England and France from the Middle Ages to the Present*, Oxford: Blackwell.

Mintz, S.W. (1985) *Sweetness and Power: the Place of Sugar in Modern History*, New York: Viking.

Monsarrat, A. (1973) *And the Bride wore . . .: the Story of the White Wedding*, London: Gentry Books.

Montagné, P. (1961) *Larousse Gastronomique*, English edn of 1938 French original, London: Hamlyn.

Mui, H.-C. and Mui, L.H. (1989) *Shops and Shopkeeping in Eighteenth Century England*, London: Routledge & Kegan Paul.

Mure, W. (ed.) (1854) *Selections from the Family Papers Preserved at Caldwell*, Part I, Glasgow: Maitland Club.

Nairn, C. and Strathern, A.J. (1974) *The Kawelka (Ongka's Big Moka)* (film), Manchester: Granada TV.

Napier, J. (1879) *Folklore in the West of Scotland*, Paisley: Gardner.

Newton, G. (1988) *Shades of Light. Photography and Australia 1839–1988*, Sydney: Australian National Gallery/Collins.

Nichols, D. (1978) *Marriage, Divorce and Family in Scotland*, Edinburgh: Scottish Association of Citizens Advice Bureaus.

Nirvana (1946) *Commercial Cake Decoration*, new edn, London: Maclaren.

—— (1951) *Advanced Piping and Cake Designs: Method and Application of Fine Piping and Run-in Work*, London: Maclaren.

—— (1954) *Decorated Cakes and Confectionery*, London: Maclaren.

Nott, J. (1733) *The Cook's and Confectioner's Dictionary*, 4th edn, London: Rivington.

Nutt, F. (1809) *The Imperial and Royal Cook*, London: Mathews & Leigh.

Nutt, J. (1789) *The Complete Confectioner*, London.

Oliver, G. (1832) 'Old Christmas customs and popular superstitions of Lincolnshire', *Gentleman's Magazine* CII: 491–4.

Partridge, J. (1596) *The Treasurie of hidden Secrets, Commonlie called The good Huswives Closet*, enlarged edn, London.

Pepys, S. (1970–76) *The Diary of Samuel Pepys*, 10 vols, eds R. Latham and W. Matthews, London: Bell.

Perkin, J. (1989) *Women and Marriage in Nineteenth-Century England*, London: Routledge.

Platt, H. (1603) *Delightes for Ladies, to adorne their persons, tables, closets and distillatories*, London.

Power, E. (ed.) (1928) *The Goodman of Paris*, London: Routledge & Kegan Paul.

Price, R. (1655) *The Compleat Cook*, London.

Raffald, E. (1769) *The Experienced English Housekeeper*, Manchester.
—— (1772) *The Manchester Directory*, Manchester. (Reprinted Manchester: Sutton, 1889.)
Richards, A.I. (1939) *Land, Labour and Diet in Northern Rhodesia*, London: Oxford University Press for International African Institute.
Richardson, S. (1753–54) *The History of Sir Charles Grandison*, 7 vols, London.
Rogers, C. (1884) *Social Life in Scotland*, vol. I, Edinburgh: Grampian Club.
Rombauer, I.S. and Becker, M.R. (1973) *Joy of Cooking*, revised edn, New York: New American Library.
Rorer, S.T. (1902) *Mrs Rorer's New Cook Book*, Philadelphia: Arnold.
Rundell, M.E. (1824) *A New System of Domestic Cookery*, new edn, London: Murray.
Sahlins, M. (1976) *Culture and Practical Reason*, Chicago: University of Chicago Press.
St. James's Chronicle (1799) VI, April 16–18.
Samuel, R. and Thompson, P. (eds) (1990) *The Myths We Live By*, London: Routledge.
Sandys, W. (1833) *Christmas Carols Ancient and Modern*, London: Beckley.
Schülbé, E. (1898) *Cake Decoration*, Glasgow: Maclaren.
Scott-Moncrieff, R. (ed.) (1911) *The Household Book of Lady Grisell Baillie, 1692–1733*, Edinburgh: Scottish History Society.
Selden, J. (1726) *Uxor Ebraica*, reprint in his *Opera Omnia*, vol. II, of original of 1646, London.
Seligson, M. (1974) *The Eternal Bliss Machine*, London: Hutchinson.
Shaw, C. and Chase, M. (1989) *The Imagined Past: History and Nostalgia*, Manchester: Manchester University Press.
Shawcross, J.T. (1978) 'The names of Herrick's mistresses in *Hesperides*', in R.B. Rollin and J.M. Patrick (eds) *'Trust to good verses': Herrick Tercentenary Essays*, Pittsburgh: Pittsburgh University Press.
Sherwood, Mrs J. (1884) *Manners and Social Usages*, New York: Harper.
Sinclair, T. (1987) ' "All styles are good, save the tiresome kind": an examination of the pattern of stylistic changes occurring among silver candlesticks of the eighteenth century', in I. Hodder (ed.) *The Archaeology of Contextual Meanings*, Cambridge: Cambridge University Press.
Skuse, E. (1893) *Complete Confectioner*, 10th edn, London: Bush.
Smollett, T. (1771) *The Expedition of Humphrey Clinker*, London.
Somerville, T. (1861) *My Own Life and Times 1741–1814*, Edinburgh: Edmoston & Douglas.
Soyer, A. (1846) *The Gastronomic Regenerator*, London: Simpkin, Marshall.
—— (1853) *The Pantropheon: or, History of Food, And its Preparation, from the Earliest Ages of the World*, London: Simpkin, Marshall.
Stone, L. (1977) *The Family, Sex and Marriage in England, 1500–1800*, London: Weidenfeld & Nicolson.
Sutton, A.F. and Hammond, P.W. (eds) (1983) *The Coronation of Richard III: the Extant Documents*, Gloucester: Sutton.
Suzanne, A. (1894) *La Cuisine Anglaise à la Pâtisserie*, Paris: L'Art Culinaire.
Tante Marie (1954) *Tante Marie's French Cakes and Pastries*, trans. and adapted by C. Turgeon, London: Kaye.
Tibbott, S.M. (1986) 'Liberality and hospitality: food as communication in Wales', *Folk Life* 24: 32–51.

Trevor-Roper, H. (1983) 'The invention of tradition: the Highland tradition in Scotland', in E. Hobsbawm and T. Ranger (eds) *The Invention of Tradition*, Cambridge: Cambridge University Press.

Trollope, A. (1880) *The Duke's Children*, London.

Tuleja, T. (1987) *Curious Customs*, Harmony: Stonesong.

Van Gennep, A. (1909) *Les Rites de Passage*, Paris: Nourry.

—— (1946) *Manuel de Folklore Français Contemporain: Du Berceau à la Tombe*, 2 vols, Paris: Picard.

Vanaise, A. (1928) *Quelques Notes pour Servir à l'Histoire de la Pâtisserie et de la Crisperie*, Brussels.

Vercoe, B. (1973) *The Australian Book of Cake Decorating*, Australia: Hamlyn.

—— (1976) *Cake Decorating*, London: Souvenir Press.

Vine, F.T. (1894) *Practical Pastry: a Handbook for Pastry-bakers, Cooks and Confectioners*, London: Hampton.

—— (1897) 'Cakes and how to make them', *British Baker* XIV: 68.

—— (n.d.) *Cakes and How to Make Them*, London: Maclaren.

Wallace, E. (1975) *Cake Decorating and Sugarcraft*, 3rd edn, London: Hamlyn.

Watson, K.J. (1978) 'Sugar sculpture for grand ducal weddings', *Connoisseur* 199: 20–6.

Weaver, W.W. (1988) 'Introduction', *The Confectioner's Art*, American Craft Museum.

—— (1990) *The Christmas Cook: Three Centuries of American Yuletide Sweets*, New York: Harper Collins.

Wells, R. (1890) *Ornamental Confectionery*, London: Crosby, Lockwood.

Werlim, O. (1915) *The American Cake-Baker*, New York: Gregory.

Wheaton, B.K. (1983) *Savouring the Past: the French Kitchen and Table from 1300 to 1789*, London: Chatto & Windus.

White, F. (1932) *Good Things in England*, London: Cape.

Willy, T. (1891) *All About Piping*, London: Willy.

Wilson, C.A. (1973) *Food and Drink in Britain from the Stone Age to Recent Times*, London: Constable.

Wilson, M. (1972) 'The wedding cakes: a study of ritual change', in J.S. LaFontaine (ed.) *The Interpretation of Ritual*, London: Tavistock.

Withals, J. (1608) *A Dictionarie in English and Latine for Children and Young Beginners*, London.

Wolley, H. (1664) *The Cook's Guide: or, Rare Receipts*, London.

Young, M. and Wilmott, P. (1973) *The Symmetrical Family*, London: Routledge & Kegan Paul.

Index